BIG RIGS
IN ACTION

Robert Genat

Motorbooks International
Publishers & Wholesalers

Dedication
To Gregory Stein, M.D.,
who showed us the meaning of family,
love, and hope.

First published in 1997 by Motorbooks International Publishers & Wholesalers, 729 Prospect Avenue, PO Box 1, Osceola, WI 54020-0001 USA

Motorbooks International books are also available at discounts in bulk quantity for industrial or sales-promotional use. For details write to Special Sales Manager at the Publisher's address

Library of Congress Cataloging-in-Publication Data

Genat, Robert.
  Big rigs in action/Robert Genat.
      p. cm. —(Enthusiast color series)
  Includes index.
  ISBN 0-7603-0345-2 (pbk.: alk. paper)
    1. Tractor trailer combinations—Pictorial works. I. Title. II. Series.
TL230.12.G45   1997
629.224—dc21   97-13150

On the front cover: Most big rig drivers love the freedom of the road and are out on the open road—night as well as day—seeing the world and transporting the goods we use everyday.

On the back cover: It takes quite a bit of skill to drive a big rig like this Peterbuilt. The transmissions are all manual shift with at least nine forward speeds. Big rig transmissions are not synchronized, therefore the driver must double clutch when shifting.

On the frontispiece: The Peterbuilt emblem on this big rig suffers from a case of "road rash," the result of thousands of miles on the highway.

On the titlepage: Fuel farms run day and night, year round, to service the needs of a mobile America.

Edited by Anne McKenna
Designed by Todd Sauers

Printed in Hong Kong

Contents

Acknowledgments

First and foremost I must thank the many anonymous and unidentified truckers whose big rigs grace these pages. Their beautiful machines bring this book to life.

Thanks to my good friend Bill Scully, owner of Los Angeles Freightliner, for giving me the grand tour of his facility and for introducing me to Claire Lopez, upon whom I relied as one of my many technical consultants.

Many thanks to all the nice folks at United States Truck Driving School. Jim Dancy, Director of Market Development, gave me hours of his time answering specific questions about trucking. Anytime I called, Jim gave me his full attention and clearly articulated the business of driver training and trucking. It was with his assistance that I was able to get behind the wheel of a big rig. Also, thanks to the following folks at the United States Truck Driving School: John Nichols, Vice President of the Western Region; Elliotte Fajardo, Director of Training; and Hector Serrano, my driving instructor.

I must thank both Patricia Yasui of the California Trucking Association and Suzanne Hess of the American Trucking Associations for much of the statistical data in this book. Both Jacqui Luty and Anne Middleton of Qualcomm deserve a thank you, too. Thanks to Mandy Andreopoulos of Rockwell Automotive, Daniel Jarboe of BEALL Corporation, John Sommer of Kidron Inc., Richard Vander Woude of Superior Concrete, Tom Wickenhauser of Caterpillar Engine Division, Larry Chupp of the Mountain Water Ice Company, and John Daley of Daley Construction. I must also thank Sergeant Gary Smith and Inspector Tom McIlravy at the California Highway Patrol truck inspection facility in San Onofre, California, for their time and information. Thanks to Krista Martin of Prime Inc. for putting me in touch with Barb Jasper. Thanks to Tom Brown, owner of Sierra Pacific West, and their big rig driver/photographer Willy Moss. Finally, thanks to the following photographers for sharing their big rig images with me for this book: Fred Pushies, Kenny Gerber, Paul Harder, and Bette Garber.

Introduction

Before you start reading this book, stop for a minute and look around the room you're in. Virtually everything you see has been shipped by truck, including this book. Trucks are part of our everyday lives more than we realize. We've become dependent on trucks and on the trucking industry for the cars we drive, the food we eat, the roof over our heads and the construction of the roads we travel. Trucks provide efficient transportation of the products we buy and manufacture. Trucks serve every community in America and seventy-seven percent of all communities are served exclusively by trucking.

Today we see more and more trucks on the road. One reason is a business philosophy known as "just-in-time." Just-in-time is a process whereby goods are delivered near the time they will be used. For example, tires delivered to an auto manufacturing plant will be installed within a day of delivery on cars running down the assembly line. The goal of the automaker is to reduce the stockpile of goods he has to warehouse and pay for prior to the assembly of a car. With just-in-time, the car may be delivered to the consumer before the manufacturer even receives the bills for the components used to build it. It's an elegant concept and when executed properly, it saves money and time. The efficiency of the trucking industry is the major reason just-in-time works so effectively.

Television and the movies have often depicted the American

truck driver as a loose cannon, roaming the highways at warp speed running down any car, motorcycle, or pedestrian in his way. This image is far from the truth. Today's big rig driver is a trained professional and today's modern trucks are technically superb. Engines, refrigeration units, and even some transmissions, are computer controlled. The cabs are filled with satellite communications, on-board computers, electronic driver's logs, and electronic trip information recorders—trucking's equivalent to the flight data recorders found on aircraft. Operating this type of machine takes skill and dedication.

Big rig drivers are some of the safest drivers on the road. Mile for mile, truck drivers have an accident rate less than half that of car drivers. Between 1994 and 1995, overall highway fatalities increased 2.8 percent, while truck related fatalities went down 4.7 percent. Since 1979, truck related fatalities have decreased 27 percent. From 1984 to 1994 fatal accidents involving big trucks have been reduced by 34 percent, while miles driven has increased 37.5 percent. Recent studies have shown that of the approximately 40,000 highway deaths each year, 87 percent involved accidents between vehicles other than trucks. Of the 13 percent involving trucks, 71 percent were the fault of the car driver and 10 percent were determined to be the fault of both the car and truck driver. The remainder of the fatal accidents, including single vehicle truck accidents, can be attributed to trucks. This works out to about 4 percent of the overall fatal accident rate. This is rather low when considering the more than 152 billion miles annually traveled by the United States trucking industry. Today, alcohol use by truck drivers is almost nonexistent. Only 1.3 percent of those truck drivers involved in fatal accidents were found to be intoxicated, compared to 19.2 percent of car drivers. Testing for substance abuse is now part of being a trucker. The legal blood alcohol level for a truck driver is 0.04, half that for a passenger car driver.

Today's big rig drivers are men and women (approximately 30 percent) dedicated to safe truck operation. They have passed the written, physical, and driving tests required for them to legally slide up into the seat of a big rig. Almost all of today's drivers have attended a professional truck driving school to acquire their skills. Once hired by a company, trainees continue alongside an experienced driver before they are assigned to a rig of their own. An experienced driver can earn up to $60,000 a year, and a husband and wife team can earn upwards of $100,000 per year. Also, many big rig drivers own their own trucks. These owner/operators have made a financial commitment to invest in their own rig and to contract their own hauls. Although this is a bigger gamble, it can often deliver much higher returns.

Here are some other facts you should know about trucking. Commercial trucks make up only 10.5 percent of all registered vehicles on the road. They pay $8.4 billion in federal highway-user taxes annually. That figure represents 44 percent of the $19.4 billion in total federal highway taxes. Currently, the average amount of state and federal tax on a gallon of diesel fuel is 43.33 cents a gallon, compared to gasoline, at 36.8 cents a gallon. The trucking industry employs nearly 9 million people throughout the country in jobs relating to the trucking industry, including 2.9 million truck drivers. The trucking industry includes 360,000 companies of which 82 percent are small businesses operating six or fewer trucks. The American trucking industry annually generates $362 billion in gross revenues—78 percent of the nation's freight bill. American truckers haul 5.5 billion tons of freight, representing 55 percent of all freight volume. Predictions for the trucking industry for the year 2004 say that truckers will drive 197 billion miles, hauling 11.6 billion tons of freight.

Today, the American trucking industry operates more than 4 million trucks, each weighing more than 10,000 pounds. Since 1982, the fuel efficiency of heavy duty trucks has improved over 30 percent, largely due to advances in truck design, new engine technology, proper driving techniques and improved maintenance. The trucking industry is the second largest user of retreaded tires—about one-million a year. Recycling tires creates an enormous savings in the energy and petroleum used to make new tires.

In less than ten years, a big rig driver can cover one million road miles—an amount that would take eighty years for the average passenger car driver to attain. The big rig driver has the privilege of seeing the sun rise and set in every imaginable part of the country. They are lucky enough to see the bright lights of America's big cities from coast to coast. Every driver has a story to tell about a character they met along the road, a sight they saw, or a city they visited. Truck drivers experience life first-hand from the best seat in the house—the driver's seat of a big rig in action.

Chapter 1

Truck Tractors
Pulling in Style

The business end of any big rig is the truck tractor. A tractor is the vehicle used to pull a trailer. The truck tractor is also built to carry part of the load it's drawing. There are two basic types of tractors: the cab-over engine and the conventional. The cab-over has a flat front and the engine is placed below the cab. The conventional tractor has an engine covered by a hood placed in the front of the cab.

Cab-Over Tractors

The cab-over tractor, often called a COE (cab-over-engine), has a very distinctive wide flat front face. The name cab-over comes from the fact that the cab is located directly over the engine. A cab-over, with its forward driver seating position, gives the driver maximum road visibility. Because it's shorter than a conventional tractor, the cab-over is more maneuverable. Because of this extra agility, most cab-overs make local deliveries to large retailers and manufacturers. These local delivery cab-overs don't have a sleeper due to their short runs. They may also have few, if any, aerodynamic devices on the roof, since much of their driving is done at lower speeds.

There's no mistaking what kind of tractor is coming your way when the owner has added a large Peterbuilt logo across the grille of his truck.—*Caterpillar Engine Division/Paul Harder*

The cab-over was very popular prior to 1982, when regulations were eased regarding the overall allowable length of a tractor-trailer combination. A cab-over design tractor could be as much as ten feet shorter in length than a conventional tractor. This ten foot savings could then be used in added trailer length to haul more goods.

Another benefit of the cab-over design is the accessibility for maintenance. The entire cab is hinged in the front just above the bumper. This allows the cab to be rotated forward 90 degrees, giving mechanics full access to the engine, transmission, engine bay accessories, and all chassis components. This ease of access decreases the time it takes to do most maintenance.

There are, however, some drawbacks to a cab-over tractor. First, the ride is rough. The driver sits directly over the front wheels which transmit each road jarring bump directly up into the cab. And because the driver is placed at one end of the tractor, rather than in the middle between the axles, there is no flexing of the frame to absorb some of the road shock. Many cab-over designs offer an air-suspension for the cab to smooth out the ride.

Because the cab is positioned directly over the engine, interior space is reduced. The doghouse-sized engine bay tunnel creates a large divider between the seats, making movement difficult within the cab. Access to a sleeper, if so equipped, is also a challenge because of this raised tunnel. Some of the newer cab-overs have tunnels with reduced height, but there is still a sizable hump over the engine. Navistar has taken the lead in flat-floor cab-over technology with the 1995 release of their Flat-Floor 9800 cab-over. Before long, most truck manufacturers will be offering a similar package.

Engine noise in the cab is also a problem with a cab-over tractor, even though the undersides of the tunnels are well insulated. When taking the rig in for maintenance, the cab-over owner must remove everything from the cab and sleeper that's not permanently attached before the cab can be tipped forward. Climbing up into a cab-over is a little more difficult than getting into a conventional tractor. With the driver's door placed directly over the front tire, the foot hold steps are either in front of or behind the tire. So to enter the cab, the driver must climb at an angle around the tire while climbing vertically up to the seat. Finally, the cab-over driver sits only inches away from the front of the tractor, making this the most dangerous seat in the house in the event of an accident.

Jose Martinez owns and drives this 1990 Peterbuilt. His conventional tractor has all the elements big rig fans have come to love: a long hood, exposed chrome air filter, and chrome exhaust stacks. The fuel tank is slung alongside the frame rail just below the sleeper. On top of the sleeper is a roof fairing.

This Kenworth is typical of the new generation of aerodynamic conventional tractors. All corners have been rounded and smoothed. There are no exposed air filters or exhaust stacks to break the flow of air over the tractor's body. Even the outside mirrors have a rounded back. This particular model has a high-rise sleeper with a small fairing on the top matching the height of the trailer.

Conventional Tractors

Conventional tractors are designed with the front wheels, engine and the engine hood in front of the cab. This has been the standard, or conventional, configuration of cars and trucks since the twenties. Conventional tractors are extremely popular with big rig drivers today. There is something about the look of this design that appeals to nearly everyone. Conventional tractors also have the look of a 1930s-era car. This nostalgic look has been popular with hot rods and Harley-Davidson motorcycles for years.

With the cab placed amidships between the axles, the ride of a conventional tractor is more comfortable than the ride of a cab-over. The cab of a conventional tractor is narrower than that of a cab-over, but the floor is flat. There is also a safety factor with the conventional's front mounted engine.

There are two separate looks to today's conventional tractor. The classic conventional still carries its geometric lines and angles in the design of the cab and fenders. The classic versions also feature dual cowl-mounted air filters, bright twin exhaust stacks, and polished saddle-mounted fuel tanks. Then, there is the new smoother look for the conventional. In this design, traditional hard edges have been softened and rounded in the name of aerodynamics. The long hood is still there, but its top edge slopes downward to cheat the wind. Every corner has been radiused and blended. Every accessory that was previously attached to the exterior of the tractor has been moved under the skin, out of the flow of the air stream. Small aerodynamic changes to the exterior of a truck can make a noticeable difference in fuel mileage, and that's important to the long-haul trucker.

Fifth Wheel

Every tractor hauling a semi-trailer has a fifth wheel. A fifth wheel isn't one that rolls on the ground, but is the fixture on the tractor that provides the mechanical connection between the tractor and the trailer. It was invented in 1919 by John Endebrock and its name comes from the days when trucks had only four wheels. The fifth wheel is located behind the cab on top of the frame rails. It is made of steel, and is semi-circular in shape with a keyhole shaped slot facing rearward. The top of the fifth wheel (usually covered in grease) is called the skid plate. Here rests the weight of the trailer. The kingpin on the

This conventional Freightliner tractor is pulling a dry bulk tanker. Behind the cab two air brake lines (red and blue) and the electrical connection can be seen going from the cab to the trailer. Just above the tractor's rear wheels, attached to the frame, is the fifth wheel, the mechanical connection between tractor and trailer.

Cab-over engine (COE) tractors are boxy in appearance. The driver sits on top of the front wheels with an excellent view of the road. The big advantage of a cab-over is the increased maneuverability due to the shorter length of the tractor.

Preventative maintenance will keep a big rig engine on the road for as many as one million miles before an overhaul is needed. This driver has just filled up with fuel and has tipped the hood forward on his International to check the oil level on the big Caterpillar diesel engine.—*Caterpillar Engine Division/Paul Harder*

trailer slides up into the slot and is locked by the fifth wheel's coupler jaws. The fifth wheel must be strong enough to support the static weight of the trailer and the dynamic forces applied to it as the tractor-trailer travels down the road.

The process of hooking up is done as the tractor backs up under the trailer. On some tractors the fifth wheel is adjustable, fore and aft. This gives the driver the ability to balance the load of the trailer across the tractor. For example, if the fifth wheel were fully rearward, more trailer weight would

rest on the tractor's rear wheels. This shift in weight would reduce the weight on the front wheels and could create a dangerous handling condition. Conversely, an increase in front tire load would occur if the fifth wheel were in the full forward position. It is extremely important that the fifth wheel is properly located, fore and aft, in order to balance the weight properly and ensure safe handling of the tractor-trailer combination. As with many items on a big rig, the fifth wheel is a simple design that works.

The heart of any tractor is its diesel engine. Here, a technician is inspecting a Caterpillar 3406C 425 horsepower engine prior to delivery of this new Peterbuilt tractor. The rust colored cylinder below his right hand is the exhaust turbine side of the turbocharger.—*Caterpillar Engine Division/Paul Harder*

This Freightliner cab-over is pulling a large custom trailer built to haul race horses. Cab-over designs are typically not the most aerodynamic, but this tractor features some of the latest tricks to cheat the wind–rounded corners on the cab and bumper.

Tractors that do not have a sleeper on the back of the cab, like this cab-over Peterbuilt, are often called "day cabs." These tractors are used in daily operation hauling local loads, like this flat-bed filled with flattened cars.

Buying a Big Rig

For the person buying a tractor today, the choices are almost limitless. But, it's not as simple as walking into a Chevrolet dealership and ordering a car. When someone buys a Chevy, they usually have the choice of one or more optional engines, all manufactured by General Motors. Most of the components in that Chevy will have been manufactured by General Motors or by one of their suppliers.

When a customer walks in to a Peterbuilt, Freightliner, or any other truck dealership selling Class 8 trucks, the process is much different. Once the customer has chosen one of many basic models, the process continues by specifying the desired heavy duty mechanical components, such as engines, transmissions, axles, and brakes. All of these components are supplied to the truck manufacturer by several manufacturers who specialize in these components. The customer can chose from several different diesel engines in a variety of horsepowers. The transmission choices are as diverse as those for engines. Choices are also made for axles, suspensions systems, and brakes, all supplied by manufacturers specializing in these components. Building a truck by component selection is standard in the industry.

The cost of a new big rig tractor can run from $60,000 to $100,000. The difference in cost depends on the major components selected and the accessories added. Warranties on the powertrain are typically 3 years or 350,000 miles. This may vary with the components selected. Exterior sheetmetal warranties are typically five years or 500,000 miles. Frames are warranted for six years or 750,000 miles.

Engines

A couple of decades ago, many people thought the big rig's diesel engine was on its way to extinction because it couldn't be sanitized enough to satisfy clean-air proponents. But engineers worked long and hard, pressured by looming regulations and competitive pressures to develop the diesel. They redesigned components of the basic diesel engine and added electronic engine controls which, along with cleaner burning fuel, have produced engines that are more powerful, more fuel-efficient and cleaner-running than ever. Another benefit of these new generation diesel engines is that they last longer than ever, too. Big rig diesel engine life to its first overhaul is typically between 700,000 and one million miles.

This conventional Freightliner model is called a mid-roof sleeper cab. From the windshield back, its cab roof is raised and blended into the roof of the sleeper. Added above the sleeper is a fiberglass fairing that blends with the top of the trailer. The saddle mount fuel tanks are covered with a fairing that blends into the front fender and runs the length of the tractor. All of these modifications to the basic conventional tractor are intended to improve the aerodynamics.

Two tankers are filling up with some of Sunoco's finest that will soon be delivered to a nearby filling station. The conventional tractor on the left is a Mack, one of the oldest and most respected names in trucking.—© *Fred Pushies*

Almost all big rig diesel engines are inline six-cylinder with turbo-chargers. The displacements range from 10 to 16.4 liters (610-998 cubic inches). While there are other V-type diesels, the inline six is the most popular. It's less costly to manufacture and easier to maintain. There are three major companies that provide diesel engines to the major tractor manufacturers: Detroit Diesel, Cummins, and Caterpillar. When someone orders a new tractor, these are the choices. Mack and Volvo also build their own proprietary engines.

The phrase "more power" has certainly been an axiom for the diesel engine industry. In the mid-eighties, the average horsepower of all Class 8 engines was under 330 horsepower. By 1990 that figure had risen to 340 horsepower, and by 1995, 370 horsepower. As of this writing, the biggest of the big is the Caterpillar 3406E. This bad boy boasts 550 horsepower at 2100rpm with an awesome 1,850 pounds of torque at 1200rpm. Caterpillar makes no bones about this engine's power and has nicknamed it "The King of the Hill." Over the past few years, Caterpillar and Cummins have been 'dukeing it out' in a horsepower fight reminiscent of Detroit's muscle car era.

Something you see very little of today is thick clouds of black smoke belching from a tractor's stacks when it accelerates. This clean burning is due to electronic engine controls. These ECMs (Electronic Control Module or Engine Control Module) precisely meter fuel and its injection into the cylinders. This preciseness results in a 15 percent fuel savings over mechanically fuel-metered and injected engines. ECMs are also programmable. The engine's power curve can be slightly altered to suit the needs of the owner. A "sweet spot" can be fine tuned. The sweet spot is the rpm range where a tractor's diesel engine produces the most power and greatest fuel efficiency. The sweet spot on most ECM-equipped diesels is between 1500 and 1700rpm.

ECM units gather information from sensors reading coolant temperature, oil temperature, coolant level, throttle position, intake manifold air temperature, fuel pressure, turbo boost, and vehicle speed. The ECM units can also interface with other electronic gear to give the driver an in-cab real-time read-out of trip information, such as miles per gallon and average miles per hour. This gives the driver a tool to manage his driving for maximum efficiency. Maintenance managers can extract information such as length of trip, average miles per gallon, total

This International conventional stands out with its bright yellow paint and polished aluminum wheels. When ordering a new truck, customers make choices from a wide range of options, including engine, transmission, brakes and paint scheme.—© *Bette S. Garber/Highway Images*

trip running time, total fuel burned, gallons burned at idle, time spent in cruise control, time spent over a specific mile per hour, top speed during a trip, highest rpm during a trip, number of panic stops, and miles driven since the last oil change.

Drivers themselves are responsible for the trend toward more powerful engines. Any big rig driver will attest that it's much more satisfying to drive an adequately powered big rig. Pulling a hill in an underpowered, fully-loaded big rig is hard work for the driver. It entails a lot of shifting to maintain a safe speed. Time wasted by feeble acceleration and poor hill climbing ability results in low productivity. Fleet operators want to retain their seasoned drivers and one way to do that is to provide them with an engine with enough pulling power for the heaviest loads.

Transmissions

All big rigs are equipped with manual transmissions with at least nine forward gears. The transmission allows the rig to accelerate smoothly while carrying a heavy load. It allows the diesel engine to work within the most efficient range of its power band. Each gear in the transmission has a maximum speed determined by the engine's governor. The job of the driver is to smoothly accelerate through each of the gears. This is a rather difficult task due to the many types of transmissions, their varied shift patterns, and the lack of synchronized transmissions.

Each driver must take the time to learn the transmission in the tractor. The shift pattern is usually displayed somewhere on the instrument panel, but getting the feel of the shifter under road conditions is another thing altogether. One driver said, "You can take two identical trucks, but each one will have its own feel. You've got to get in 'em and drive 'em for a while to get comfortable."

The lack of synchronizers in today's big rigs requires the driver to double clutch for each shift. Once learned, this skill allows easy, crunch-free shifting. Veteran drivers can shift without using the clutch, but this is hard on the transmission. The latest in transmission technology for today's big rigs is the semi-automatic transmission. The driver must still use the clutch to start and when stopping, but this new generation of transmission frees the driver from using the clutch when shifting.

One of these new transmissions is the Rockwell Engine Syncro Shift (ESS). The ESS system automatically synchronizes the transmission by matching engine rpm speed to the vehicle's road speed. The HI and LO range shifts are automated as well. This transmission also features a "brake torque" feature. With this feature the driver can downshift while keeping his foot on the brake. With a standard transmission, the driver must double clutch when downshifting. To do this properly, the driver's right foot is needed on the throttle to raise the engine rpm to match the road speed. The brake torque feature allows the driver to keep a steady force on the brake pedal and use the engine's compression to augment stopping power.

The components that make up the system are: the system on/off switch and Intent switch, both on the shift knob; a speed

Each axle on this Peterbuilt tractor and its twin dry bulk trailers is fitted with its own air braking system. The engine has an air pump that supplies air pressure to the entire system. Air brakes provide the most economical and efficient method of braking for big rigs.

The diesel engines in today's tractors are 15 percent more fuel-efficient than just a decade ago. This increase in efficiency is due to electronic engine controls and precise fuel metering. The front fenders and hood are a one-piece design molded out of fiberglass. Access to the engine on this conventional Freightliner is done simply by unlatching the nose piece and tilting it forward.

sensor on the transmission's output shaft; a neutral position sensor in the transmission's top cover; and electro-pneumatic solenoids in the transmission. The system switch simply turns the ESS system on or off. In the OFF position, the transmission operates as a conventional transmission. With the system switch in the ON position, all the driver needs to do is flip the shift intent switch to the UP position for upshifting or to the DOWN position for downshifting. If the ESS system switch is turned off, the shift intent switch acts as the HI/LOW range selector.

The ESS collects data from each component switch and sensor and relays this information to the engine's ECM. The ECM processes the information and adjusts the engine's fuel delivery system to increase or decrease engine speed to match the road speed.

Brakes

The safe operation of a big rig ultimately rests on its braking ability. The engine may run poorly or may use too much oil. The fenders may need paint and the seats may be worn. But the brakes *must* be in good condition or the driver's life and those of other motorists are in jeopardy.

The most important system on a tractor is the braking system. When the test for the Commercial Drivers License (CDL) is given, an automatic failure results for errors on questions about the braking system.

The brakes on a big rig differ from those on a car. Big rigs use air, rather than hydraulic pressure, to actuate the brakes. Brakes on a big rig are also almost exclusively drum brakes, as opposed to the disc brakes you may have on your car.

The brake pedal on the floor of a big rig looks like a standard brake pedal. But when applied, the sensation is completely different. There's no "feel" to the pedal like there is in your passenger car. There is no difference in the amount of pressure it takes to apply the pedal one-quarter or all the way to the floor. The brake pedal in a big rig is simply a valve that directs air to the brake system. Pressure on the brake pedal opens an air valve. There is also a slight time lag between the time the pedal is depressed and when the rig starts to slow down. The big rig driver adjusts braking by sensing the manner in which the truck is slowing. This is not an easy task. The amount of pedal needed to stop an empty big rig is much less

than what's needed to stop a fully loaded truck. The experienced driver is able to stop the rig smoothly, whether it's loaded or empty.

The air brake system is made up of many components. A belt-driven air compressor on the engine provides air to the reservoir on the tractor and to the reservoir on the trailer. This compressor provides the air volume and pressure for the entire system on both the tractor, trailer, or trailers. The governor on the compressor maintains air pressure between 85 and 130psi. Standard safe operating pressures are between 90 and 110psi. Each reservoir must have the capacity to stop the truck and still maintain an additional reserve pressure if the engine quits running or if the compressor fails. A gauge on the instrument panel in front of the driver displays the system pressure. If the system falls between 75 and 55psi, a warning buzzer will sound and a red light will illuminate on the instrument panel. Both are there to warn the driver that there is a system problem.

When the driver applies the brakes, it is actually opening a valve that allows air pressure to push against the brake chamber diaphragm at each wheel. Attached to the diaphragm is a push rod. This push rod presses against a lever called the slack adjuster. The slack adjuster pivots on a shaft. At the opposite end of that shaft, which extends into the brake drum, is a small cam in the shape of an "S." When the shaft rotates, the cam applies pressure against the brake shoes, expanding them to come in contact with the brake drum, thereby stopping the truck. Adjusting the slack adjuster is the method used to adjust the brakes.

The tractor's air brake system is connected to the trailer's system by two hoses at the back of the cab. The blue hose is for the service brakes (standard brakes). The red hose is for the emergency brakes. The coupling devices are called glad hands. The glad hand connectors have rubber seals to prevent air from leaking. The hoses on the back of the cab are supported by a pole with a spring swivel base called a pogo stick. The pogo stick keeps the hoses from scraping on the tractor frame and possibly damaging them. In the area of the glad hands on the trailer is a female electrical connector. This connector provides power to the trailer's brake lights and marker lights. Making the glad hand and electrical connections takes only a few seconds.

This Peterbuilt has just pulled into a gas station to unload its tanks. This style of truck is called a straight truck, or bobtail. It's basically the same as a conventional tractor, but in the place of the fifth wheel is a permanently mounted tank. It's pulling another tanker trailer. Each of the tanks is split into two compartments, allowing this driver to carry four types of fuel.

The main reason air brakes are used on big rigs is for their power. A large, fully loaded truck with a hydraulically operated brake system would require excessive pedal pressure to stop it. Secondly, use of air brakes makes for the easy adaptability to a trailer. If the brake system were hydraulically operated, the connection time to hook up and disconnect a trailer would be excessive. The air brake system on today's big rigs is simple and very effective.

Aerodynamics

Aerodynamics are as important to a big rig as they are to your passenger car. Recently, Freightliner Corporation conducted a study and determined that at 60 miles per hour, it took 186 horsepower to move a modern tractor trailer. Aerodynamic drag accounted for the largest amount of power used—52 percent—or 97 horsepower. Rolling resistance, the effort needed to move a truck's weight down the road, required 72 horsepower. The drivetrain friction losses and engine accessories accounted for less than 10 percent of the available

horsepower absorbed. Due to the many variables in truck design, options, and configuration, manufacturers don't publish the Cd (drag coefficient). But, today's trucks have a Cd of between 0.4 and 0.6. By comparison, a new Corvette has a Cd of 0.29. Let's take a look at what's being done today to improve aerodynamics on the modern tractor.

Three major factors affect the amount of aerodynamic drag on any vehicle: its speed, size, and shape. At speeds under 50 miles per hour, the aerodynamic forces on a large truck are about equal to its rolling resistance. As speed increases, air resistance increases exponentially. The less aerodynamic the vehicle—a tractor-trailer for example—the greater the aerodynamic impact. A non-aerodynamic tractor-trailer combination, traveling at 65 miles per hour, needs an additional 60 horsepower to maintain that speed than if it were traveling at 55 miles per hour. The size, or frontal area, of a tractor-trailer also contributes to aerodynamic drag. The frontal area is the overall square footage of the shape pushing against the air. The frontal area of a big rig pulling a van trailer is approximately 100 square

This conventional tractor has a small fairing on the roof to deflect air up and over the top of the trailer. The trailer is a refrigerated van, often called a "reefer." Modern refrigeration units, like the Carrier manufactured unit on the front of this trailer, work efficiently even when sheltered by a tractor's fairing.

feet. While the square footage of the frontal area cannot change, one thing that can be changed is the shape of the tractor.

During the past ten years, much has been done to re-design the shape of trucks in order to "cheat the wind." To-day's conventional trucks have hoods with steeper angles. The lower the front edge of the hood, the less interrupted the flow of air. Tractor bodies are more rounded, especially around the fenders, bumper and headlights. Some manufacturers have added valences which curve under the bumper to smooth the air flow. Windshield angles have gotten steeper to work har-moniously with the angle of the hood. Tractor windshields will probably always remain a two-piece flat design due to the fre-

quency of replacement and the lower cost of flat glass. Most cab-overs now have a curved glass edge panel on each side. Streamlining tricks also include recessed door hinges, door handles, and steps. Even the exterior mirrors and their brack-etry have been reshaped in an effort to slice through the wind more effectively.

Probably the most dramatic change to the appearance of tractors has been the addition of aerodynamic fairings. These fairings range from a simple add-on to the roof, to a complete set of fairings that change the overall appearance of the truck. Roof fairings are the most common. They have been shown to reduce drag by as much as 25 percent. Roof fairings are most

The Top Fuel Dragster style wing on the roof of this Peterbuilt may not help the aerodynamics much, but it looks cool. Above the grill shell is a small, Plexiglas bug deflector. Its job is to deflect the air stream and bugs away from the flat windshield panels. The owner of this tractor has added a few accessories such as a cab mounted spotlight, a row of vertical amber lights near the external air filter, and some tasteful pin-striping on the hood.—© *Bette S. Garber/Highway Images*

effective on a van type trailer. When pulling a tanker or flatbed, they are less effective and, in some cases, can worsen the overall aerodynamics. The earliest and most simple roof fairings were hollow add-on caps. With the current popularity of the high-rise sleepers, roof fairings are now molded into the sleeper's construction. To be fully effective, the roof fairing must blend smoothly and tightly with the front of the trailer. If there is too large a gap between the rear edge of the roof fairing and the leading edge of the trailer, much of the aerodynamic efficiency will be lost. The greater the gap, the greater the drag. This is especially true in a cross wind condition. A well-designed roof fairing can improve fuel efficiency by as much as 14 percent—a good investment for the long-haul trucker.

Becoming more popular today are chassis fairings. These panels are constructed from Fiberglass or plastic and are attached to the side of the tractor to cover the fuel tank and step area. The chassis fairings smooth the air flow between the front wheels and the drive wheels. They are most effective in a crosswind situation. An additional benefit of chassis fairings is the reduction of wheel spray in wet conditions.

However, there have been some problems associated with side fairings. Maintenance on these panels is an added cost to the truck owner. Side fairings are more susceptible to damage due to their low road level location and proximity to the tires. The side fairings also restrict access to certain components, making routine maintenance more time consuming and costly. Some owners feel the side fairings limit cooling air flow to the transmission and clutch, thereby increasing operating temperatures. This limited air flow may also have a negative effect on brake life, due to increased temperatures.

Just how much can aerodynamics help the average long-haul driver? Mack Truck engineers did some calculations using

This cab-over is pulling a 53-foot dry freight van filled with loaves of bread. With a trailer full of bread, this big rig is probably well within the 80,000 pound weight limit set for a tractor-trailer combination. Attached to the cab of the tractor is a large fairing. Its aerodynamic benefit is only marginal, because of the large gap between it and the trailer.

one of their CH613 conventional trucks pulling a total weight of 80,000 pounds. They simulated a run between Allentown, Pennsylvania, to Martinsburg, West Virginia. The first run was done with a basic tractor and trailer with no aerodynamic devices, cruising at an average speed of 61 miles per hour. The miles per gallon averaged 5.77. When they added a roof fairing and chassis fairings, the miles per gallon jumped to 6.50, a savings of 12 percent. That may seem like a small amount, but the average long-haul driver covers 120,000 miles a year. A 12 percent increase in mileage equates to fuel savings of almost 2,500 gallons!

Tires & Wheels

Tires also have an effect on fuel economy. Most of the tires on today's big rigs are radials. Bias tires are used in certain applications, but carry up to a 6 percent fuel mileage penalty. Bias ply tires typically have six to eight diagonal plys, while the radial tire has only one ply, plus a series of belts. The more plies a tire has, the greater the internal friction and the more heat it generates. Tubeless tires also roll more efficiently than tube types. The tread pattern is also a factor in mileage. The two most common tread types are ribbed and block. Block type tires are most commonly used for traction in snow and mud. This penalty for increased traction is approximately 5 percent in fuel economy.

One of the biggest factors to tire life and fuel economy from tires is their inflation pressure. A 30 percent under-inflation will incur up to a 5 percent fuel mileage penalty. Also, under-inflated tires are the most common cause of "alligators"—the truck tire remnants we occasionally see strewn along the highway. It is a common misconception that these tire pieces are from a failed recap. In fact, the tire you see laying there may have been a brand new tire. The major cause of "alligators" is under-inflation. A severely under-inflated tire will generate a tremendous amount of heat and will eventually fail–whether new or recap. One of the most important things a big rig driver can do is check tire pressures weekly with an accurate gauge. (In the old days, tires were checked with a billy club. A properly inflated tire has a unique "ring" to it when struck, whereas an under-inflated tire will respond with a thud. This method of checking tire pressure is no longer valid for the modern trucker).

More and more big rigs are rolling on aluminum wheel rims today. The change is not just cosmetic; there is a very practical reason. A full set of aluminum wheels on an 18-wheeler will save almost 600 pounds over conventional steel wheels. This allows for an additional 600 pounds of freight to be carried—more freight, more money. A secondary benefit of aluminum wheels is the reduction in unsprung weight. This results in an improved ride and better handling characteristics. And, one final benefit—aluminum wheels look great.

Sleepers and Other Accessories

Attached to the cab of any long haul tractor will be a sleeper. A sleeper is a compartment that gives a driver a place to get some rest. The earliest sleepers were a simple berth behind the cab. But today's sleepers have grown into much more. A majority of sleeper-equipped tractors are factory equipment. Truck manufacturers are providing features that were found only in custom sleepers a few years ago. Tractor manufacturers stop short of installing bathroom amenities. The extra cost for the plumbing of

Big rigs with columns of black smoke belching from the stacks is a vanishing image. Today's trucks are equipped with electronically controlled engine management systems that give the driver a very powerful engine (up to 550 horsepower) with outstanding mileage and low emissions.

RV-like features is not something the average fleet buyer is willing to pay for. Many drivers discretely slip a porta-potty under their bunk for an open road emergency. But, most drivers are accustomed to using public facilities along the highways.

Sleepers come in sizes from 36-inches deep to a maximum of 74-inches deep. The heights vary from a low ceiling–extension of the top of a conventional's cab–to a full raised roof that will allow a six-footer to stand comfortably. The raised roof sleepers typically incorporate a roof fairing into the design. There are two different design philosophies for sleepers on today's big rig: semi-integrated and integrated.

The semi-integrated sleeper is an add-on to the rear of the truck's cab. The rear of the cab is cut away and the sleeper added on. The advantage of this design is that the sleeper can be removed when the tractor is turned-out from long-haul to short-haul work, where a sleeper is not required.

The integrated sleeper is built on as part of the cab with no wall separating the cab from the sleeper. The absence of a separating wall gives the illusion of more interior space. This single unit cab-sleeper is a less complex design, but does not allow for the removal of the sleeper.

The sleeper compartments on the modern big rig are efficiently designed. Built-in storage spaces, computer desks, reading lights, and convenient pre-wired TV antenna hook-ups are just a few of the modern sleeper's amenities.

Some long-haul truckers have opted for custom sleepers. These folks—often a husband and wife team who may spend four to five weeks on the road with the kids and pet—have all the comforts of home built in. The cost of this home-away-from-home can range as high as $65,000. The list of amenities is lengthy and some may surprise you. Most have a microwave oven or hot plate installed, but some owners install a two-burner electric stove. To keep the food fresh, a small refrigerator or refrigerator-freezer combination is typically installed. Bathroom amenities range from a porta-potty to a traditional commode. Water for the custom sleeper ranges from cold only, to both hot and cold. And, if you have hot water, why not have a shower? The biggest drawback to a shower in a sleeper is not the space the shower stall requires, but the volume of water (40 to 80 gallons) that must be carried. Other built-ins you might find in a custom sleeper include: a sound system, TV/VCR, computer, central vacuum, and satellite TV. Power for these extras is generated by an inverter or accessory AC generator.

25

Chapter 2

Trailers
Haulin' the Goods

Trailers are the cargo carriers of the team and there are many types of trailers designed to carry every conceivable type of load. Two basic types of trailers are used today: the semi-trailer and the full-trailer.

The semi-trailer is the most common and is distinguished by having rear axles only. When hooked up to a tractor, the front is supported by the tractor's fifth wheel. When not hooked up to a tractor, the semi-trailer uses its landing gear to maintain a level setting. A semi-trailer's landing gear consists of a pair of vertical legs on which the forward end of the semi-trailer rests when not attached to a tractor. Landing gear are permanently mounted to the frame of the trailer. They contain pads called "feet" which are retracted when the trailer is hooked to a tractor. The only semi-trailers without landing gear are low-bed and pole trailers. The semi-trailer cannot roll on its own and must be hooked to a tractor.

Under the front of every semi-trailer is a kingpin. The kingpin is a short cylinder of steel that locks into the tractor's fifth wheel. The kingpin is set under the front of the trailer on a large steel structural plate. This plate rides on the fifth wheel and supports the weight of the front half of the semi-trailer.

This Peterbuilt is pulling two trailers (a double) loaded with hot asphalt. He is laying down a windrow that the paver will pickup and lay down evenly on the road.

This Freightliner is pulling a horse trailer that was built in 1962. The cupola on the rear of the trailer is where the stable boys ride while transporting horses. There's a button in the cupola that's hardwired to a buzzer in the cab in case they need to communicate with the driver.

When a semi-trailer is not connected to a tractor, it rests on its landing gear.

Full-trailers have axles at both ends. These axles support the trailer's full weight. Full-trailers are used as the second trailer in a "double" (two trailers with one tractor) and as the third trailer in a "triple" (three trailers with one tractor).

Semi-trailers can be converted to full-trailers with the use of a converter dolly, often called simply a dolly. A dolly is an axle with a fifth wheel on top and a draw bar on the front. When slid under a semi trailer, the trailer's kingpin is locked into the dolly's fifth wheel and the drawbar is attached to the rear of the trailer ahead of it. It takes more driving skill to drive a double or triple. Backing with a double or a triple, except for very short distances, is virtually impossible.

Each trailer has its own set of air brakes and electrical wiring. Connections attached to the tractor provide the necessary air and electrical power.

Here are some of the more common trailers you will see rolling down a highway near home.

This trailer is a dry bulk tanker with a capacity of approximately 16,000 cubic feet. This type of tanker is used to haul peletized products and grain. The product is loaded through hatches on top, and unloaded with the assistance of air pressure through discharge ports in the bottom.

This sleek looking International tractor is pulling an acid tanker which can be easily identified by its small diameter and stiffener rings encircling the tank. Diamond-shaped placards are placed on each of the four sides to denote the type of hazardous material being shipped.

This end-dump trailer is being filled with the remnants of asphalt road that is being removed by a profiling machine. The machine and truck move forward in unison while the conveyor fills the trailer. Once fully loaded, the truck will pull ahead and the driver will manually pull the tarp (rolled tightly at the front of the trailer) over the trailer. This prevents any of his load from blowing out of the trailer when he reaches highway speeds.

Vans

The most common style of truck trailer is the van. It's a simple, rectangular box-shaped trailer seen every day on the road. Vans are used to transport dry freight and are also called dry freight vans. Dry freight is anything that needs only to be covered from the elements when transported. Therefore, dry freight can be anything from corn flakes to cash registers. Many vans display the company's name on the truck to take advantage of free advertising as it rolls down the road. Other companies don't want to draw attention to their cargo. Few

would want to steal a truck filled with breakfast cereal, but if that van were filled with Harley-Davidson motorcycles or video cameras, the chances of it being stolen or high-jacked increase. Most companies shipping goods that can be easily turned for a profit on the street, use the stealthy approach and transport in an unmarked van.

Van lengths vary from 20 to 53 feet. The shortest units, with single axles, are used for city deliveries because of their maneuverability. Often two, 27-foot trailers are connected to make a double. Larger vans, with lengths from 35 to 53 feet, are usual-

At first glance this trailer may look like a typical dry freight van, but it's actually a shipping container often called a sea-land container. These containers are hauled by ship, stacked on top of each other. At the pier, they are lifted out of the ship by crane. When transported by truck they are loaded onto a trailer frame designed specifically to haul that size container.

ly used singly. Van construction is typically a steel frame, wood floor, and a box constructed of aluminum. The load floor of a dry freight van is flat. This flat floor allows fork lifts to load and unload cargo on pallets. Maximum capacity is approximately 2,800 cubic feet, with a payload capacity of up to 50,000 pounds.

A warehouse van (often called a furniture van or a drop van) looks very similar to the dry freight van. The exceptions are the drop-floor and the addition of side doors. The drop-floor extends down as much as 27 inches. The dropped portion starts just aft of the coupler and runs to the rear of the trailer. The drop floor increases the trailer's total capacity to over 3,000 cubic feet. A lower dropped floor results in less steep ramp angles. This makes loading and unloading with dollies and hand carts much easier. The drop floor is not entirely flat, as in the dry freight van. Wheel houses protrude into the cargo area at the rear axle locations. This is typically not a problem, since this type of van is seldom loaded with a fork lift.

An electronics van looks very similar to the warehouse van. It too has a drop floor, but with a maximum drop of 21 inches. The electronics van is equipped with smaller 15-inch diameter wheels, instead of the 20-inch wheels used on the warehouse vans. These smaller wheels, smaller wheel houses

A typical sight in any neighborhood is a moving van, or furniture van. These vans are designed with a low load floor to accept more than one household's furnishings. Side doors allow easy access when parked at a curb in a residential area.

In the moving business, you have to hustle! All goods are loaded by hand or with the use of a small hand cart like the one this young man is using. The ramp has a non-skid surface.

and shallower drop, allow for a flat load floor. Electronics vans can be as long as 53 feet in length and have a capacity of 3,100 cubic feet.

This trailer type was designed to haul computers for the electronics industry. The flat floor allows the use of fork lifts to load and unload. Electronics vans are also equipped with air-ride, or soft ride, suspensions to protect the delicate cargo. Because of their extra cubic foot capacity, these vans are also used to haul what is known as "balloon freight." Balloon freight is anything high in bulk, but low in weight, such as potato chips, toys, or clothing.

Reefers

Refrigerated vans, commonly called "reefers," are essentially insulated dry freight vans with a refrigeration unit hung on the front. Refrigerated vans are the same size and capacity as dry freight vans, but insulation is added to the walls and roof. A refrigeration unit (reefer) is added to the front of the van. It's a self-contained refrigeration unit powered by a small four-cylinder diesel engine. The fuel for the reefer's diesel is contained in a small tank under the trailer. The cold air from the unit flows into the van through simple duct work that runs along the ceiling. The floor of the van is ribbed to allow increased circulation of air around the cargo.

Prior to loading the van, the driver will start the reefer unit and set the thermostat for the desired temperature. This pre-cools the van. Pre-cooling removes the residual heat from the van body and gives the product being loaded better protection. It is important that the product being shipped is at the correct temperature when it's loaded. Drivers should always check the temperature of the product as it's being loaded. Reefer units are only designed to maintain the temperature of a product when it's loaded. They are not designed to cool a warm product.

The use of pallets is highly recommended when loading a refrigerated van. This allows air to freely move around and through the load. The lack of good circulation can cause hot

The inside of a moving van has a wooden floor. The ceiling is marked to designate the cubic foot capacity. The framework on the side is for attaching racks that could form a platform to hold a shipper's personal car. Prior to loading the van, it is filled with packing materials and padding.

Previous Page
Fuel farms provide a centralized location for the distribution of gasoline. This Texaco tanker is being filled prior to a delivery to a local filling station. The network of red-tipped vertical pipes hanging above this truck is a fire suppression system.

spots and top-freeze. The way the products are stacked is another important factor in maintaining correct cooling. Fruits and vegetables are stacked to allow air to freely flow through the product. This is called "air-stacking." Products like meat and frozen foods, which do not create heat, are stacked in the center of the van. All products must be stacked away from the walls. This will insure sufficient air flow and prevent any heat filtering through the walls from affecting the temperature of the shipment.

Modern reefer units are controlled by a microprocessor to maintain a constant temperature. Each unit has a lighted display panel on the driver's side of the trailer. From the cab, the driver can monitor this panel by looking in the side mirror. Here are some common temperature settings (in degrees

This beautiful gold-over-white Freightliner COE is powered by a Detroit Diesel engine rated at 475 horsepower. It is pulling a 40-foot Fruehauf flat-bed trailer stacked with 47,000 pounds of 2X4s. Each group of bundles has two sturdy straps holding them to the trailer. The owner's pride is evident by the way this spotless rig sparkles.

This 1995 Freightliner is attached to an insulated tanker containing 6,300 gallons of hot asphalt. The driver is looking down an open hatch as the tank drains its contents. The insulated tanker maintains the asphalt's temperature between 300-400 degrees Fahrenheit.

Fahrenheit) for transporting certain goods: ice cream, -20°; frozen meats and seafood, -10° to 0°; frozen fruits and vegetables, 0°; ice, 15° to 20°; dairy products, 33° to 38°; fresh meats and seafood, 28° to 32°; fresh fruits and vegetables, 33° to 38°; and bananas, 55° to 60°.

A reefer unit can also provide heat to the trailer. If the outside temperature drops below the reefer's thermostat setting, the reefer unit will provide heat to the trailer. Imagine a load of fresh vegetables coming out of California's Imperial Valley in December. It's loaded into the reefer on a day when the temperature is near 70°. Its destination is Chicago. Over

Right
Fuel tankers can have up to four separate compartments in one trailer. This allows the truck to carry and deliver several grades of gasoline at one time. This driver has connected his tanker to two underground tanks and is letting gravity take care of the unloading. Notice how the reflective tape strips on the side of this trailer stand out.

the next three days on the road, the outside temperatures may vary from 85° across Arizona, to well below zero in the Chicago area. The reefer unit will keep the vegetables from cooking in the desert and freezing in the mid-west by maintaining the trailer's interior at a constant temperature.

You may notice a small door on one of the two large rear doors of a refrigerated van. This door allows the driver to look in and check the load. When transporting certain vegetables, like tomatoes, which give off gases, this door serves as a vent and may be left open.

One of the newest innovations in refrigerated vans is a trailer with a compartmentalized interior. The trailer's interior can be divided into as many as four separate compartments, all with different temperature requirements. This type of trailer

Self contained refrigeration units hung on the front of trailers are called "reefers." This Carrier-built unit has been opened up to reveal a four-cylinder diesel engine that runs the refrigeration unit. Fuel for this engine is kept in a tank under the trailer.

Below
This 1981 Peterbuilt conventional tractor needs all of its Caterpillar-generated 450 horsepower when hauling a load like this Caterpillar D8L dozer. The combination tractor-trailer totals 105 feet in length. The trailer is constructed of three sections; the front is called a jeep, the center is the trailer, and the rear is a booster. This configuration is called a "nine axle" for the number of axles in the combination of tractor and trailer. Ground clearance on a loaded trailer is between four and six inches.

allows a single truck to carry a mixed load of frozen vegetables, fresh meat, and dry freight, to make one stop at a small convenience store. These three different loads would otherwise have required delivery by three different trailers, due to the load's temperature differential.

Containers

Another type of van used to haul dry freight is the overseas dry freight container or sea-land container. It's unique because the van body, or container, is separate from the chassis. It's attached to the frame by large pins in each corner of the van. These containers are typically found around the waterfront, since they are transported by ship. With this type of trailer, the entire van body is loaded onto a trailer chassis. A company shipping a product overseas will load the container at their factory or warehouse. It will be transported by truck to the shipyard, where it will be loaded onto the ship or held to be loaded onboard.

Tankers

Tanker trailers are built with a single compartment or are segmented into as many as four compartments. The single compartment tankers can be either baffled or clean bore. Baf-

When driving a refrigerated van, the driver monitors the reefer's cycle by looking in his left-hand door mirror. There he will see this lighted panel mounted on the refrigeration unit. With a quick glance, the driver can tell which cycle the unit is in and if the set temperature is being maintained. Some refrigerated trucks have an alarm in the sleeper to warn the driver if the temperature is out of range.

fles, dividers built into the tank, are designed to keep the load from surging. Baffled tanks are much more difficult to clean out because of the internal corners and joints that may trap some of the contents when unloading. The internal welds on most tankers are ground smooth and polished in order to reduce the chance of any of the load sticking inside. Clean bore tanks drain easily and are easy to clean out. Some loads, like milk, must be transported in a clean bore tanker. Otherwise, the movement of the milk against the internal baffles would churn it to butter. Large tankers can be split

When ears of corn are transported to a canning plant, they're hauled in a bulk trailer. The trailer's rear door has been opened and the ears of corn are starting to fall out as the hydraulic lift raises the front of the trailer.—© *Bette S. Garber/Highway Images*

This pair of dry bulk tankers is used to haul cement powder. The tanks are fabricated from aluminum and are of welded construction. The rear trailer is a full trailer, able to roll on its own without the aid of a tractor to support the front end.

into several compartments to carry several different grades of gasoline.

Liquid tankers carry a wide variety of goods such as petroleum, acids, chemicals, food, and even ordinary water. To handle these various liquids, tankers are built out of steel, stainless steel, and aluminum. Coatings are often applied to the inside of the tank to withstand certain chemicals. Tankers can also be insulated to hold the temperature, hot or cold, for an extended period of time. Liquid tankers are built in two basic shapes: cylindrical and elliptical. The cylindrical shape is

Left
This slick blue Kenworth conventional is pulling a simple dry freight van. It is being filled with packaged flour from this flour mill. Dry freight vans are the most common trailers seen on the road.

the most versatile and the strongest. The elliptical tankers have the advantage of a lower center of gravity. Tankers are designed to haul as much as 10,500 gallons of liquid. The controlling factor for the number of gallons in the load is, as always, the combined weight of the tractor-trailer which cannot exceed 80,000 pounds.

Other specialized liquid tankers are used to carry acids, liquefied gases, and other materials which must be kept at a certain temperature. Acid tankers have a smaller diameter tank with a series of external stiffener rings which encircle the tank. Acid tankers have a variety of internal coatings designed to resist the acids they carry. Liquefied gas tankers are cylindrical in shape with rounded ends. They are designed to carry oxygen, propane, butane, and other gases in their liquid state. Insulated tankers look very similar to a standard liquid tanker. Internally, they have an insulated tank which maintains the temperature of the product. Insulated tanks are especially useful in transporting liquid asphalt.

Tankers used to carry loads other than liquids are called dry bulk tankers. These tankers carry powder or pelletized products, both edible and non-edible. Edible products transported include sugar, powdered milk, grains, and flour. Examples of non-edible goods carried in a dry bulk tanker are cement, dry chemicals, pelletized plastics, and limestone. Dry bulk tankers provide an efficient means of transporting products that otherwise would have to be bagged and hand-loaded.

Dry bulk tankers are usually clean bore tanks built in the shape of cone called a hopper. The conical shape directs the product toward the discharge outlet. Small dry bulk trailers may have only one hopper. Larger trailers may have as many as four hoppers.

Dry bulk tankers are unloaded with the assist of air pressure. The tanks are pressurized (approx. 10psi) to blow the contents out through the discharge line. Air pressure is also used to agitate the product in the hopper to facilitate unloading.

Flat-bed Trailers

Flat-bed trailers, often called platform trailers, are used to haul loads that don't need protection from the elements, or that are too large to be loaded into a van trailer. At the front end of a flat bed may be a header board, often called a "headache rack." A header board is a vertical plate attached to the trailer which prevents the load from shifting forward into the cab in case of a sudden stop. Tarps are commonly used to cover loads on the flat bed trailer.

Low Bed Trailers

Low bed trailers, also called gooseneck trailers because of the shape of the forward portion of the trailer, are the "heavy weights" of the trailer world. Low beds are used for specialized loads which are either very heavy, very large, or both. Low beds can haul loads weighing up to 100 tons. They are used to haul bulldozers, cranes, transformers, jet engines and just about any other commodity that is too large or too heavy for a standard trailer. To be able to handle larger loads, many different axle and tire combinations are used on the low bed trailer. Some low beds have outriggers which, when extended, give an extra foot of width on each side of the trailer. On some low beds, the front gooseneck portion of the trailer can be disconnected to allow the bed to drop to the ground. This facilitates the loading of certain pieces of heavy equipment. A majority of the loads transported on low beds are "permit loads." These loads are allowed to travel certain routes at certain times, by virtue of a special permit.

Other Trailers

Other trailers typically seen include pole trailers, livestock trailers, bulk grain and bulk fruit trailers, and dump trailers. Pole trailers are made up of two segments. The front portion attaches to the fifth wheel and the rear section has the wheels to support the load. The portion in between is a telescopic pole. Pole trailers are most commonly used to transport cut trees and telephone poles.

Livestock trailers are used to transport animals on the hoof such as cattle, sheep, and pigs. These trailers resemble a van except the sides are reinforced to support the movement of the animals. The sides are also slotted to allow air to circulate and keep the animals cool. Some trailers that ship smaller animals have two decks.

Bulk grain and fruit haulers are similar to an open-top van except the sides are lower. The open top facilitates loading by a chute. These trailers will often have top bows that support a tarpaulin. This tarp restrains the load when going down the road. Dump trailers are used to haul soil, gravel, and sand. These trailers are most often seen at construction sites being loaded by an excavator to haul away excess fill. These trailers frequently have tarps to keep debris from falling out onto the roadway. There are two basic styles of dump trailers: end dump and bottom dump, often called "belly dump." The bottom dump trailers have doors underneath the trailer which open and allow the load to be emptied. End dump trailers have a telescopic hydraulic front lift which raises the front of the trailer so the contents can slide out the back. End dump trailers have been called "suicide wagons" because they will occasionally tip over during dumping, taking the tractor over with the trailer. The tractor and trailer must be on level ground before the driver raises the body. Level ground is difficult to find at most construction sites. Sometimes, even on level ground, the trailer will tip if part of the load sticks to the inside of the body as it's being raised.

Markings

In December 1993, new National Highway Traffic Safety Administration (NHTSA) rules were put in place regulating the marking of new cargo trailers weighing more than 10,000 pounds and with a width of more than 80 inches. Studies indicated that tractor-trailers marked with reflective tape were 20 percent less likely to be rear-ended. The new standard encourages the use of red and white reflective sheeting (the technical name is retroreflective tape) over the plastic reflectors. This new sheeting is approximately ten times brighter than the old style plastic reflector and the sheeting reflects light at much greater angles. This new standard can be met

Refrigerated vans look similar to dry freight vans. They often have a side door for easy access. This particular trailer has a roll-up rear door; other refrigerated vans may have dual swing-open doors.—*Kenny Gerber*

with the plastic reflex style reflector, but the advantage of the tape is ease of application and durability.

The sheeting, in 2-inch wide strips, 18 to 48 inches long, is to be placed along the length of the side of a van between 15 and 60 inches from the pavement. These strips are also placed on the rear of vans. Continuous 2-inch wide horizontal strips are to be placed on the rear of the trailer with an additional 1.5-inch wide strip placed on the rear horizontal underside guard (commonly called the "ICC bumper"). Also to be added to the rear of the trailer are 2-inch wide white reflective strips in an "L" shape. These are to define the upper corners of the trailer. These "L" shaped strips are to be added to the top corners of tractor cabs and sleepers, too.

The design of the trailer type places limits on where the new markings can be placed. Exempt from the standard are specialized trailers such as pole trailers and sea-land cargo containers. These containers are considered cargo, although at first glance, they resemble vans.

When this standard was introduced, there was a lot of discussion over the color and placement of the tape. Many felt that colors other than red should be used on the side of the truck. To the average driver, red means the back of a vehicle— not the side. Others favored colors that would harmonize with their company's logo, but the NHTSA stood firm on the red and white strips. Their position was that the markings would eventually be recognized by all motorists as those of a big rig.

Aerodynamics

Aerodynamic improvements are not for tractors alone. When properly designed, improvements to trailer aerodynamics can improve fuel efficiency by as much as 5 percent. One of the most common aerodynamic devices for trailers is the bubble-nose added to the front of a van to smooth the air flow. Side skirts are also being seen on trailers. They, like the tractor's side skirts, are most effective in a cross wind situation. Undercarriage dams have been added to improve airflow. Rear door frames have been redesigned to reduce some of the suction created by the large flat rear plane of the trailer. The manufacturers of both tractors and trailers are working together to improve the aerodynamic combination without sacrificing their compatibility.

Interstate Highway System - Lifelines Across America

The 44,546 mile U.S. Interstate Highway System recently celebrated its 40th birthday. Former president Dwight D. Eisenhower was the early visionary of the project. In 1919, as a young Army officer, Dwight Eisenhower was given the assignment to determine how important the nation's highways were to national security. His road trip from Washington D.C. to San Francisco took two months, over mostly uncharted dirt roads and broken-down bridges. Later, as an Army General in World War II, Eisenhower saw the importance of Germany's Autobahns to their war effort. On June 29, 1956, while serving as president, Eisenhower signed legislation that created the Dwight D. Eisenhower System of Interstate and Defense Highways—known today as our Interstate Highway System.

This system of roads criss-crossing continental America is laid out in a clear-cut pattern. All Interstate highways with odd numbers indicate north-south routes. These odd numbered Interstates begin on the West Coast (I-5, San Diego, California, to Seattle, Washington) and increase in number going east, with the highest numbers on the East Coast (I-95, Miami, Florida, to Houlton, Maine). Three digit numbers such as 405, 435, or 787 are offshoots that route traffic off of the Interstate around a major metropolitan area.

The even-numbered Interstates are east-west highways. Even-numbers begin small at the southern border and increase going north, with the highest numbers at the northern border. The lowest numbered Interstate highway in the continental United States is I-4 which is not a true interstate, but runs entirely within the state of Florida from the Tampa-St. Petersburg area to Daytona Beach. The Interstate that crosses the nation from east to west along the southern border is I-10. It starts in Jacksonville, Florida, and runs west continuously to Los Angeles, California. At the top of the country is I-94 with connections to I-90. That route will take you from Seattle, Washington, east to Chicago, Illinois, where I-94 continues to Detroit, Michigan, and I-90 splits to go to Buffalo, New York.

Chapter 3.

Driving a Big Rig

To haul cargo with a big rig, the driver needs a CDL (Commercial Drivers License). The CDL is not a separate driver's license, but an endorsement to the standard state driver's license. On April 1, 1992, every truck driver in the country was required to meet minimum standards to operate a commercial vehicle. These standards were set forth in the Commercial Motor Vehicle Safety Act of 1986. This act required everyone who wanted to drive a commercial vehicle to be tested for proficiency in truck safety and driving skills.

Prior to the establishment of the CDL, an unscrupulous driver could acquire a license from several different states to drive a truck. If the driver obtained too many points against one license, the driver could give that one up and still have others to drive with. There were no computers linking the driver's record from state to state. This meant there were multiple driving records in multiple states for the same person. Today each person has only one driving record. This license information is stored on computer for 55 years and can be accessed in any state by any law officer.

The driver of this tanker is right where he should be—in the center of his lane. Due to the width of a tractor-trailer combination, a split second lapse in the driver's concentration can have him crowding the adjacent lane.

Possessing a CDL is like owning a Gold Card. It's not easy to get and one mistake can get it taken away. One of the best ways to obtain a CDL is by attending a professional truck driving school. It's not necessary to attend a school, but these schools have the knowledge and the equipment to get you on the road in the shortest amount of time.

To drive a big rig hauling cargo across state lines, the driver must be at least 21 years old. When a potential driver applies for a CDL, the driver signs a form which authorizes testing for drugs and alcohol. If the prospective driver does not sign that form, a CDL will not be issued. The prospective driver must get a physical exam to prove that the driver is physically fit to drive a big rig. This physical identifies any medical condition that may interfere with the safe operation of a commercial vehicle. Every two years, a driver possessing a CDL must go through the same physical. The physician also issues a Medical Certificate Card to the driver which he must carry when driving. If this card has expired the driver will receive a citation.

There are several written tests which must be passed by the applicant. There is a 50-question general knowledge test taken by all CDL applicants. There is a 20-question test for those applicants who will be driving a combination vehicle, i.e. a tractor-trailer. An air brakes test (20 questions) is taken by all applicants who will be driving a truck with air brakes. If the prospective driver will be driving combinations (two or three

Instructors, teaching students how to alley dock a big rig, stand with their left hand on the tractor's front fender and their eyes on the rear of the trailer. The instructor communicates verbally with the driver, giving instructions on where he should look and how much he must turn in each direction. The alley dock is one of the more difficult skills a big rig driver needs to master.

trailers), transporting hazardous materials, or transporting liquids in bulk tankers, the driver will be required to pass a written 20-question test for each of these.

Next, the applicant is tested on the pre-trip inspection of the tractor and trailer. Prior to climbing up into the cab of a big rig, the driver is required to inspect the tractor and trailer for safety defects. During this inspection, the driver must touch or point to the item being inspected and tell the CDL examiner what he is inspecting, why he is inspecting it, and what that item would look like if it were unsafe. Part of this inspection is done in the cab with the prospective driver in the seat behind the wheel. The driver must know what each gauge reading should be and what each switch is for. The driver is required to

know the air pressure governor cutout. The driver also must demonstrate how to check for low air pressure warning devices. Failure to perform an air brake check is an automatic failure. Only after passing the pre-trip inspection will the applicant be allowed to proceed to the skills test.

The skills test demonstrates the student's ability to handle a big rig at slow speeds in typical driving situations. The course for the test is laid out with traffic cones. The prospective driver must be prepared to pass the following tests: forward stop, straight line backing, alley dock, measured right turn, and backward serpentine. The forward stop requires the driver to smoothly stop the tractor-trailer at a designated line. The straight line backing tests the driver's ability to keep the

This double (two trailers) of cement powder is affectionately called a "powder train." The funnel shape of the trailers places much of the weight toward the top, raising the center of gravity. This high center of gravity necessitates lower cornering speeds to reduce the chance of rolling over.

trailer within a 12-foot wide lane while backing. The alley dock tests the driver's ability to back a trailer up to a loading dock which is at a 90° angle from the normal traffic lane. The measured right turn requires the driver to make a right turn and have the trailer's rear wheel come within six-inches of a rubber cone placed on the course. The backward serpentine test has the driver backing through a course of three cones set in a line. Failure of any skills test will end the test and the prospective driver will not be allowed to continue to the driving test.

The driving test is done on the road with the prospective driver behind the wheel and the examiner in the passenger seat. The prospective driver will follow a route specified by the examiner, simulating most of the driving conditions a truck driver will encounter. It includes left and right turns, intersections, railroad crossings, curves, up and down grades, rural roads, multi-lane urban streets and highway driving. The examiner carefully watches how the driver handles each situation and may ask questions along the way. After driving under an overpass, the examiner may ask the prospective driver what

One of the skills a driver must exhibit when testing for a commercial drivers license is the alley dock. The driver of this Ford conventional has executed the maneuver perfectly and is about to have his trailer unloaded at this food store.

the posted clearance or height was. The examiner may also ask what the posted weight limit was on a bridge just crossed. The way to pass this portion of the test is to follow the examiner's directions without question, to drive smoothly, and to drive safely. The best way to fail this portion is to get stopped for a moving violation or be involved in an accident—it has happened.

It is possible to lose the CDL driving privilege. The laws are very strict regarding driving under the influence and leaving the scene of an accident. With the first conviction comes a one year suspension of the CDL. If the driver is hauling hazardous material and is convicted for driving under the influence or leaves the scene of an accident, the suspension is for three years. A subsequent conviction will result in a lifetime suspension. If a big rig is stopped and a law officer detects *any level* of alcohol, the officer can place that vehicle out of service for 24 hours. Professional drivers do not drink and drive.

What it's Like Behind the Wheel

Driving a big rig is not as easy as you might think. In fact, it's extremely difficult. I was lucky enough to be invited to the United States Truck Driving School's facility in the high-desert community of Victorville, California, to drive one of their big rigs. Their school, with its closed driving course, is located on the site of the former George Air Force base. I wanted to know what it's like driving a big rig, and therefore wasn't required to do any of the pre-trip inspections required by their students. I climbed up into the driver's seat of their Freightliner with instructor, Hector Serrano, who took the passenger seat. Attached behind was a 48-foot van trailer. The first thing I noticed was how comfortable the seat was—lots of up and down springing to dampen the roughest road. I grabbed the large diameter steering wheel and looked out across the drooping hood of the conventional Freightliner. The view to the front and to the left is excellent from the high vantage point of the driver's seat. This seating position makes you feel as though you are in total command.

Outside mirrors are the driver's only view to the rear. This Freightliner has one large standard mirror and two wide-angle mirrors. When turning a big rig, the driver spends as much, or more, time looking in his mirrors to watch the back of the trailer as he does looking in the direction of travel.

This livestock trailer has three cargo levels for the pigs that are being transported. Animals have a high center of gravity. To reduce the center of gravity of the trailer as much as possible, it is loaded from the bottom up. The animals are also contained as much as possible to keep them from moving around and affecting the trailer's balance.—© *Bette S. Garber/Highway Images*

The first thing I wanted to feel was the stiffness of the clutch. I put my left foot on it and pushed, expecting it to be easy—it was as stiff as a 1960s era muscle car. With the clutch in, Hector showed me the shift pattern for the nine-speed gear box. At about 2 feet tall, the shifter was sticking straight up out of the floor in perfect position for my right hand. There is no ball-shaped knob at the top, but rather a cylindrical grip. At the front of the grip is a switch that's used to shift the transmission between ranges. When the driver shifts into fifth gear, he flips the lever up. That pre-selects the higher range for the next shift back to the location of second gear. Second gear location is now sixth gear. The shift pattern is the conventional "H." First gear (full left and back) is actually a creeper gear. I

will be starting in second, which is found by taking the shifter and pushing it forward from its free position with no sideward force. With the clutch depressed, I got the feel of the shifter and where the gears were. The pattern was close and the shifter felt solid.

This is it. I'm ready to go. Hector has me check the air pressure to be sure we have brakes. He looks nervous with an amateur at the wheel. I push the transmission into gear and start to let out the clutch. Hector informs me there is no need to touch the accelerator; the idle speed of 500rpm is all you need to get it rolling. The clutch starts to take hold and we're moving. Hector informs me that there is no reason to ride the clutch. "As soon as you are moving, you can

Again, I let out the clutch without touching the accelerator pedal, all the time fighting the instinct to give it gas and ride the clutch. A better start this time—but not great. I drive straight ahead and inform Hector I plan to turn right at the orange rubber cone placed ahead. Hector suggests I start my turn when the cone, visible out the window to my right, is even with the cab. I start turning the large wheel. It takes little physical effort to turn the large wheel. Its large diameter keeps me reaching for more wheel to make the turn. Hector is telling me to watch my mirrors. Watch my mirrors? I'm just trying to keep the tractor from hitting anything! Watching the mirrors is one of the most important things to do when driving a big rig.

The tractor is only there to drag the trailer along behind it. That dragging trailer, as long as 53 feet, is the problem. One of the skills tests for a CDL is the measured right turn, where the driver must come within six inches of a cone without running it over. My right turn was far from measured, as I ran over the cone. Hector is holding back his laughter. He explains to me that on the streets, that cone could have been a pedestrian

When delivering sand and gravel to this cement plant, drivers position their bottom dump trailers over a grate. A conveyor below transports the load into the areas at the left of the frame.

let it out all the way," he says. I do and we are slowly creeping ahead.

Before I go too far or too fast, I want to get the feel of the brakes. I depress the clutch and apply the brakes. My first sensation was that there were no brakes, since there is no feeling of pedal pressure. Then the truck shuddered to a sudden halt. Hector braced himself to keep from hitting his head on the windshield. Between the delay of the air brake system and lack of pedal feel, I think smooth braking would be a tough thing to learn.

The driver of the Peterbuilt is keeping an eye on the air pressure gauges as his load of cement powder is being unloaded. Air pressure at 10psi is forced into the tanker to loosen and force the powder out. It takes about 45 minutes to empty both tankers.

It takes quite a bit of skill to drive a big rig like this Peterbuilt. The transmissions are all manual shift with at least nine forward speeds. Big rig transmissions are not synchronized, therefore the driver must double clutch when shifting. Although tough on transmissions, many drivers have mastered the skill of shifting without the use of the clutch.

standing on the sidewalk. I try another right turn, but this time Hector talks me through it. He tells me to start turning and I ask, "Now?" He says, "No–back there where I told you."

In truck driving school, the communication between instructor and student is definitely one way—instructor to student. The student must follow the instructor's commands exactly, without question. There is no secondary set of controls for the instructor. The student has complete control of this rolling machine. Now I'm watching my mirrors and Hector is telling me how much to turn to smoothly negotiate my turn. This one's better, but not smooth. Once straightened out, I stop the truck. To stop smoothly, it takes my full concentration.

I want to feel what it's like to shift. Big rig transmissions are not synchronized like they are in passenger cars. This means the driver must double clutch when shifting. Double clutching is something I did as a kid, downshifting my 1957 Chevy's three-speed transmission that didn't have a synchronized first gear. To double clutch, you shift the transmission into neutral, let the clutch out, set the engine rpms to the level they will be at the current road speed in the next gear, push in the clutch, and shift.

Here's how it works in the big rig. I started out at 500rpm in second gear and accelerated to 1500rpm, my shift point. I depressed the clutch, pulled the lever into neutral and let the clutch out. The split between gears is approximately 400rpm,

To drive a big rig like this Freightliner, the driver must possess a Commercial Drivers License, commonly called a CDL. To obtain this license, the driver must pass written tests, pass a skills test in maneuvering a big rig, and also pass a road test. To maintain the CDL, each driver is required to take a physical to ensure that the driver is physically fit to drive a big rig.

so I needed to set the engine rpms in neutral to 1100rpm, depress the clutch and pull the lever back into the next gear and let out the clutch. The first time I missed my rpm and loudly ground the gears. I stopped and started again, hoping to get a better shift. This time I followed the instructions and the shift came off smoothly. At that moment, I was rather impressed with my trucking skills. Hector was still chuckling under his breath. I didn't want to push my luck by trying to downshift, so I slowed to a stop.

Hector asked if I wanted to try to back up. And "try" I did. I selected reverse gear by pulling the shift lever all the way to the left and then pulling back. Hector had me position my right hand on the top of the wheel at the 12 o'clock position and told me that if I pulled the wheel to the right, the trailer would go left; and conversely, if I pulled the wheel to the left, the trailer would go right. Reverse gear is extremely low and with the clutch out at an idle, we were barely moving. The mirrors are all you have when backing and they get filled with a lot of trailer

Part of the job of a big rig driver is to ensure that the load is being properly loaded and unloaded. Here, the driver at the left is watching as the fork lift operator removes two cartons of pumpkins from his truck. This trailer held a total of 44 bins, stacked two-high. Each bin weighs between 700 and 900 pounds. Pumpkins and watermelons are two vegetables that are loaded from the vine into the truck.

very quickly. I could see how a new driver could get crossed up very easily when backing. Hector asked me if I wanted to try the alley dock and I graciously declined. I'm sure he was pleased.

My short experience behind the wheel gave me a greater appreciation of what it takes to handle a big rig. It's not a passive activity. Your eyes must be constantly moving, scanning the instrument panel, the road ahead, and especially the mirrors. Old driving habits must be broken when it comes to shifting and braking. The lack of feel and the lag time in the brake pedal still makes me cringe. The entire experience has given me a much greater appreciation for those men and women who drive the big rigs.

The grader loaded on this low bed trailer could be driven short distances across public roads. For longer distances, it must be transported by truck. Extra care must be taken when loading a piece of equipment like this because of the width of the grader's tread. Only half of its tires are in contact with the trailer, which makes loading a precarious task. Once on the trailer, the grader must be chained down securely to prevent it from shifting.

Tricky Loads to Haul

Each load carried by a big rig takes some special attention to make sure it is safely transported. Certain loads are inherently more difficult or dangerous to transport. Any hazardous material always takes special care (see HAZMAT sidebar). Other loads can be dangerous, too. The height of a big rig's center of gravity is important to safe handling. A big rig with a high center of gravity can roll over if the driver has to swerve suddenly. It's very important for the driver to make sure the weight of the load is as low as possible. One load that is difficult to drive with is suspended meat hanging in a refrigerated truck. This load has a very high center of gravity, and the swinging beef carcasses create a pendulum effect when the truck corners. Dry bulk tankers also have a very high center of gravity and occasionally, when going around a corner, the load will shift. Carrying livestock can be tricky. When the animals move around in the trailer, the center of gravity shifts and makes a rollover more likely. False bulkheads can be installed to contain the animals in the livestock trailers,

thereby restricting this weight shift within the trailer.

Some live cargo on the hoof is extremely valuable and requires special care. "It's like haulin' dynamite," says Denny Waller, who has been transporting thoroughbred race horses for most of his life. "The key is to be quick and smooth. Smooth for the horses and quick, so there is plenty of air circulating around them so they don't overheat." Drivers who haul race horses prefer to haul them at night when the temperatures are lower and there is less traffic. Most horse trailers are built to carry a maximum of nine horses. Six face forward and three rearward. These are very pampered horses and the driver must know which way each horse prefers to travel, facing forward or rearward.

From the cab, an experienced driver can tell if a horse is uncomfortable or unhappy. Waller once hauled a race horse that had just been imported from Argentina. "As I was driving along, I could feel this horse kicking up a fuss. I stopped the truck and unhitched the horse. I walked it out into a field about 50 feet from the truck and the horse relieved himself—he just

Keith Campbell, a driver for the Mountain Water Ice Company, is loading a palate of ice into his refrigerated 48-foot trailer. Twenty-two palates will be loaded for a total weight of 20 tons.

The dock space at the Mountain Water Ice Company in Oceanside, California, is just wide enough for four trailers. Skills in maneuvering a big rig are critical when backing into such a narrow space.

Delivery to most convenience stores can be a difficult task because of the confined space in which to maneuver. The driver of this 48-foot reefer has positioned himself for an easy exit after unloading two containers of bagged ice. At the rear of his trailer is a hydraulic platform that allows him to roll the containers out and then drop them to street level.

didn't want to go in the truck. He was calm for the rest of the trip." Waller also said that he regularly stops to water the horses, since they are accustomed to getting a lot of attention.

Permit loads are those which are physically larger or heavier than the law allows for normal truck carriage. The transporter must get a permit from the state highway department to allow transport of certain cargo. In the application, the transporter describes its dimensions, weight, location, and destination. The highway department will designate a time of day and a route to take. A time of day is assigned that will not unnecessarily delay other normal traffic on those roads. The route is specified along roads able to withstand the weight and size of the load.

Willy Moss drives for Sierra Pacific West, a construction contractor based in Encinitas, California. His job is to haul heavy equipment from job site to job site. Moss drives a 1990 Peterbuilt with a Caterpillar 425 horsepower engine. The low-

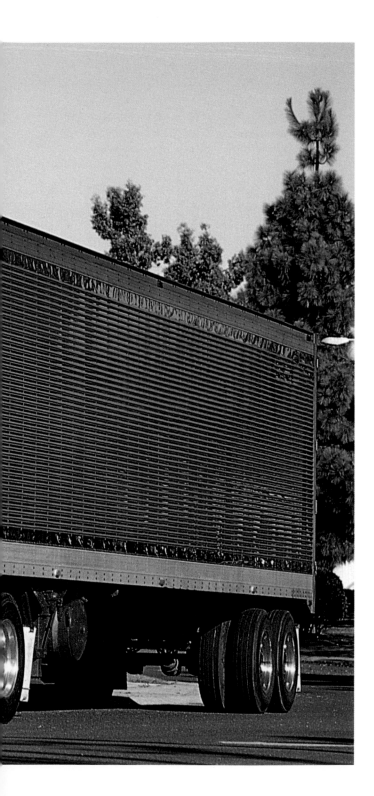

bed trailer Moss pulls is made specifically for hauling oversize loads. It has 16 wheels on two axles and has no suspension other than the rubber bushings on the suspension arms.

A pilot vehicle, car or pickup truck, escorts the big rig transporting the oversize load. The pilot vehicle has rotating yellow lights on the roof and a sign in between those lights that says OVERSIZE LOAD. The pilot vehicle leads or follows the load at the instruction of the truck driver. The truck driver and pilot vehicle driver are in constant radio communication during the trip.

Prior to loading the piece of heavy construction equipment, caked mud and debris is scrapped off to prevent it from falling into the travel lanes en-route. In California, the only two items that can escape legally from a commercial vehicle are clear water and feathers from live birds.

Today's load is a 75,000 pound wheeled dozer. Along with the 32,000 pounds for the tractor and trailer, the total weight is 107,000 pounds, well over the 80,000 limit. Before loading it onto the trailer, Moss drives the dozer around to make sure the tires are dry. Good traction reduces the chance of slipping when loading it onto the trailer. It's very important that the dozer be centered on the trailer. If it's off to one side, the load will be out of balance. Because the dozer blade is wider than the trailer, equal amounts should hang over each side. Once the dozer is up on the trailer, Moss lowers the blade against the step in the front of the trailer. This firmly plants the dozer. Next come the chains with ratchet binders to firmly tie it down. While Moss is attaching the chains, the driver of the pilot vehicle attaches red flags to the extremities of the dozer. OVERSIZE LOAD warning signs are affixed to the tractor and trailer.

Prior to leaving, Moss gives instructions to the pilot driver as to where he wants him positioned in relation to the truck. The route is direct with no stopping. Moss is restricted to the far right lane except when passing. As you can imagine, there

Each applicant for a Commercial Drivers License must perform a pre-trip inspection of his truck and trailer. Each major component of the truck is inspected with special emphasis on the brakes. The goal is to confirm that the truck is safe to drive. Safety conscious drivers inspect their trucks prior to each trip.

HAZMAT

Hazardous materials, often called HAZMAT, represent a special category of products often transported by truck. Hazardous materials are those that, by their nature, can be hazardous to the environment and to humans. There are nine categories of hazardous materials. Class1: Explosives. This includes any materials which have a mass explosive hazard, which would include projectile and fire hazard. Class 2: Gases. This includes any gas that is flammable, any compressed gas that is non-flammable, and any poisonous gases. Class 3: Flammable and combustible liquids. Class 4: Flammable solids, spontaneously combustible materials, and materials that are dangerous when wet. Class 5: Oxidizers and organic peroxides. Class 6: Poisonous and infectious materials. Class 7: Radioactive materials. Class 8: Corrosive materials, liquid or solid. Class 9 are those miscellaneous materials not covered by the other classes. And, there are some substances that are too hazardous to be shipped by truck—nitroglycerin, desensitized nitroglycerin, and diethylene glycol dinutrate.

Drivers hauling hazardous materials must have a special endorsement on their Commercial Drivers License. To get that endorsement, the driver must pass a written exam. Prior to transporting hazardous materials, the company employing the driver will arrange to have the driver attend special training classes covering the materials he will be transporting. The driver hauling hazardous materials has some extra responsibilities. The driver must make sure the shipper has properly identified and marked the shipment correctly. The driver has the right to refuse any shipments not properly prepared or if they are leaking. The driver is also responsible for the attachment of the proper hazardous materials placards on the front of the tractor and on both sides and the rear of the trailer. The driver must then, without delay, safely transport the load following all special rules regarding the type of material being transported. For instance, a driver transporting chlorine must have an approved gas mask on board. At railroad crossings, a truck transporting chlorine must stop 15 to 50 feet before the nearest rail. It can then proceed if there is no train coming, but the driver is not supposed to shift gears while crossing the tracks. Any big rig hauling hazardous materials must check the pressure, with a gauge, of any dual tires prior to the trip and every two hours or 100 miles, whichever is less. Trucks hauling explosives cannot park, except for short periods of time, within 300 feet of a bridge, tunnel, building, place where people gather, or an open fire. In California, any driver hauling more than 500 gallons of a flammable liquid is subject to a $500 fine for a first speeding offense. Subsequent penalties are stiffer. Hauling HAZMAT is no picnic.

will be no passing today pulling a total weight of over 100,000 pounds. The ride in the cab is rough. There is no suspension in the trailer and the roughness is transmitted through the fifth wheel to the tractor. Moss explains that each load rides differently. He went on to explain that the combination of road speed, road condition, wheel base of the load, the weight of the load, and the way the load is mounted on the trailer all have an effect on the ride. In addition, the ride can be affected by the type of "wheels" on the piece of equipment being hauled. A crawler with metal tracks will ride differently than a vehicle with rubber tires.

"Because of the weight, I allow a lot of space between vehicles," Moss says. "You drive to stay out of trouble and you need to anticipate what the cars are going to do." As he was telling me that, I looked to the right and watched as a small Ford van was entering the freeway. The van's driver had a map opened on the steering wheel and was not looking at the traffic with which he was about to merge—100,000 pounds of Peterbuilt. At the last moment, the driver of the van noticed the big rig and accelerated ahead. All the time Moss had his eye on that driver and was ready to move to his left if the van got any closer. Ahead on the right was a series of cement barriers on the shoulder at the edge of the freeway. The width of the dozer hung over onto the shoulder. Moss, noticing it in the distance, radioed the pilot who was following directly behind. Moss told him to slide to his left and block both lanes so he could ease the truck over, away from the barriers. Later, Moss noticed in the distance a car parked on the shoulder and gave it a wide berth as he passed.

Moss has been driving big rigs since 1970. His experience and knowledge made transporting a piece of heavy equipment seem as easy as driving a Chevy Sedan down the street.

Driving a big rig can be dangerous for a variety of reasons. Tom Shaw, of Lakeland, Florida, used to haul crude oil in Texas, driving a Mack with a tanker. He'd go out to the oil well, fill up with oil, and haul it to either a pipeline station or to a refinery. One day he stopped outside the Sheriff's office to alert them to another truck he saw get hit with a downed power line.

"I get out of the truck," recalls Shaw, "and notice a light commin' from the rear of the trailer. I walk around and it was on fire! A cap had come off the hub. All the lube had drained out, and the residual grease had caught fire. This tanker was fully loaded with crude oil. These tankers are vented to let the air in and out when you fill up and unload. These vents frequently don't seal all the way. If there was just a little bit of vapor that trickled back there–BOOM. I could just see this big fireball visible for miles with the black smoke associated with petroleum stuff. I thought about it for just a second. What do I do? Do I take off runnin' to save my neck or be a hero and risk dying. What do I do? I went in and grabbed the fire extinguisher out of the truck and started blasting this grease fire. Nothin' happened—it wasn't goin' away. So I ran across into the Sheriff's office and said, 'You got an oil tanker out here on fire! Get somebody out here right now!' The lady was just dumbfounded. I went back out and worked it a little more and was finally able to get it out by the time the fire trucks arrived."

This Peterbuilt is hauling a flat bed with pre-formed concrete. Notice how the load is spaced to each end of the trailer, directly over the rear axle and fifth wheel. Three straps firmly secure both groups of concrete sections. Proper load balance is critical to the handling of a big rig.

This double is loaded with boxes of freshly picked vegetables. The performance of a big rig differs greatly when loaded or unloaded. The driver must be able to brake his rig smoothly and safely, whether it's fully loaded or empty.

67

Trucks hauling asphalt are loaded at the plant where the asphalt is made. The driver on the left has positioned his truck under the chute and the hot asphalt is being loaded. The Peterbuilt on the right is pulling into position to be loaded. After these trucks are loaded, they will drive across scales to confirm the weight of the load they accepted.

Shaw's reaction is not unusual for today's trucker. Truckers are usually the first ones to stop at an accident to lend a hand. With the communication tools they have in the cab, they can notify local police and call for emergency services. Beyond notification, they will venture into dangerous situations to save life and limb. Big rig drivers Vincent Carr, of Pleasant Valley, New York, and Shawn Dyke of Umatilla, Oregon, pulled an unconscious driver from a pickup truck stalled on the railroad tracks with a fast approaching freight train barreling toward them. Christopher Dyson, of Rock Hill, South Carolina, rescued a driver from a burning car that had rolled over. Truckers Rob Lomanno, of Malden, Massachusetts, and Chris Kendall, of Nashua, New Hampshire, teamed up to rescue a woman and her three children from a car that had burst into flames after another had run into it. Nowhere on the CDL does heroism appear as a job requirement for driving a truck—it just seems to be the nature of the big rig driver.

Previous page
This large bottom-dump trailer was just loaded by an excavator. The driver is transporting this load to another area at the construction site where he will dump it for fill. Driving a big rig in a construction zone can be tenuous due to the uneven, temporary roads that must be traveled.

Most big rig drivers love the freedom of the road and could not sit behind a desk all day. They are out on the open road, seeing the world, and transporting the goods we use every day.

Chapter 4

Life on the Road

A big rig driver will see more of the country in one year than the average person will see in a lifetime. While there is a great deal of freedom in the job, today's trucker must live by a strict set of rules. These rules apply to the rig the driver is driving and to the time spent behind the wheel. While the driver's job is to deliver the load on time, it's also his responsibility to deliver that load safely.

Log Books

A log book is kept by any driver who drives more than 100 miles, as the crow flies, from the location where the driver normally reports for work. The log book is the driver's personal driving record, kept in 15-minute increments. It records everything from his off time, to his on-duty (but not behind the wheel) time, driving time or time in the sleeper berth. The log book is to be kept on the driver's person while operating the vehicle. Every time the driver's status changes, he must make an entry. A change in status includes any of the following situa-

One of the most interesting aspects of driving a moving van is enjoying the various destinations and scenery en route. The driver of this Atlas moving van has pulled off the road and has parked in a mall parking lot to get a bite to eat. Workers are provided by the local moving companies to load and unload the customer's household items.

Sometimes it's nice to have a good friend on the road with you, even if he can't take the wheel. Many drivers take their pets along to keep them company on long trips.

tions: driving the rig; stopping for a meal; stopping to rest or sleep; stopping to unload; stopping to pick-up a load; going home. In short, all activities must be annotated in the driver's log book.

The log book can be requested by any law enforcement officer at anytime. Every time a driver takes the truck through a roadside inspection lane, the inspector will ask to see the log book. Falsification of logs in most companies will result in a se-

vere warning or other forms of reprimand. If the falsification continues, the driver will be terminated.

The most common falsification is logging minimal time for an unload. In this situation, the driver will log an unload as taking 30 minutes, when it actually may have taken much longer. The driver then logs the difference as sleeper time—who's going to know the difference? Now the driver has more time available to drive than the law allows. A truck driver can't be on duty more than 60 hours in a 7-day period, or for 70 hours in an 8-day period. In the old days it wasn't uncommon for the driver to be two days behind on his logs. Today, if an officer catches a driver too far behind on the logs, he will shut the driver down for 24 hours. The driver is not allowed to recreate the log. Law enforcement will always err on the side of safety. The driver won't receive a violation—he'll be 24 hours late delivering his load. The impact may be no dock time available. That driver may have to wait additional hours to unload. Imagine a timed refrigerated load that needs to be delivered on time to avoid spoilage. In this situation, the freight is late and the driver is not making any money sitting still.

Inspections

On the road, one fact of life for a big rig driver is inspections. Each state has at least one truck inspection station set up along a major interstate route. This inspection station will usually house a weight station and an inspection facility. Signs along the road give truck drivers ample warning that they are approaching a weight station.

As they enter, there may be a lane for empty trucks and one or more for loaded trucks. The weights are taken with the truck rolling at 3 miles per hour. If within specifications, they are given a green light to proceed. If the truck's weight is over the limit, the driver is asked to come around again. This time, the truck will have each axle weighed individually and a print out is made. Weight laws are very complicated from state to state. In general, a truck cannot weigh over 80,000 pounds and there are weight maximums for each axle, as well.

A violation may be resolved by adjusting the fifth wheel to balance the load more evenly across the axles. Once completed, the driver is allowed to proceed. If the violation cannot be resolved, the driver must off-load material either onto the

Thirty-year big rig driver Clark Smith sits in the cab of his 1995 Freightliner talking to two other drivers prior to leaving the Swift Transport yard in Fontana, California. Smith's Freightliner is equipped with Qualcomm's OmniTRACS system that keeps him in satellite communication with his dispatcher wherever he may travel. The antenna for the OmniTRACS is the small white circular fixture on top of the sleeper fairing.

ground or onto another truck to reduce the weight to the legal limit before the driver can proceed. This often entails calling the dispatcher and having another truck sent to transfer the load—a very time consuming proposition.

In trucking, time is money. The only loads that are allowed to continue—with a violation—are hazardous materials. It is unsafe and impractical to transfer a hazardous material at a weight station. The only other loads permitted to proceed are "permit loads." These are non-reducible loads that exceed standard width, height, weight, or length. Permit loads are items that, while over the maximums, have no other way of transportation, such as a large bulldozer or an airplane.

Once a driver clears the weight station, he must roll past the inspection stations. Inspectors, often called "creeper cops," watch as the truck rolls toward them. They look for the inspection sticker on the lower outside corner of the passenger side windshield. They also look at the overall condition of the truck. If the truck has been inspected within the last 90 days (evidenced by the sticker), the inspector will not pull it over unless he sees an obvious problem with the truck (such as an air leak, bald tire, or leaking liquid). If the sticker has expired, or if there is no sticker (even if it's a new truck), the inspector has the option to direct the truck into an inspection lane.

Rolling through a weight station is part of life on the road as a big rig driver. These weight stations are set up along interstate highways in every state. The driver exits the road and rolls across the scales at 3 miles per hour. The legal weight limit for a loaded big rig is 80,000 pounds. Trucks weighing over this limit will be re-weighed to confirm the first reading. If found overweight, the driver must off-load to reduce his weight before continuing.

Inspections at these stations are performed by uniformed officers of the local highway patrol or state police, or by civilian commercial inspectors. The civilian inspectors are not sworn officers and do not carry a side arm. The Commercial Vehicle Safety Alliance (CVSA) oversees commercial truck inspections across the United States. The CVSA got together with the trucking industry and came up with a set of guidelines for truck inspections. While specific laws governing commercial vehicles vary from state to state across the United States, the drivers who enter an inspection station in Iowa will get the same inspection that they would in Kentucky or in any other state. The drivers know exactly what to expect. The form the inspector uses is similar from state to state and if they pass, they get a sticker that's good for 90 days in all states.

When driving a big rig, deliveries must be made day or night and in any kind of weather. Under the tarp on this flatbed trailer is a load of plywood. It's the driver's job to secure that tarp before starting on his trip and to remove it when unloading. It's not much fun to fold a wet tarp in a rainstorm.

Most inspectors have a set routine when they inspect a truck. First, they place a set of chocks under the front wheels. Normally, the driver stays in cab, because the driver will be required to turn the steering wheel back and forth and apply the brakes when asked to do so. The inspector then approaches the driver and asks for his license, registration, log book, and a manifest if the truck is carrying hazardous material.

The inspection usually starts with a check of all lights and turn signals. The inspector will give the brakes a thorough inspection. First, he inspects the tires, wheels, lug nuts, and examines the outside of the brake drums. He inspects the frame for cracks. All components bolted to it are checked for security. The fifth wheel is inspected for any gaps between its surface and the trailer plate. Its structure is checked for cracks or loose mounting bolts. He checks to see that the fifth wheel's release arm is in the locked position and that the locking jaws are secure. The inspector will check the rear of the frame, springs, spring mounts, and the air lines that connect to the trailer. Once the inspector completes his external checks, he slides under the truck. He will mark the pushrod on the brake actuators and ask the driver to apply the brakes. He ensures that the push rod's travel is not excessive.

"The most common violation we see here is brakes out of adjustment," says California Commercial Vehicle Inspector, Tom McIlravy. "It can be very dangerous and we're very touchy about brakes. If the brakes are too far out of adjustment, we'll put the guy out of service." This means parking the rig until it can be fixed.

The inspectors find many things about which the drivers are unaware, because the drivers seldom crawl under the truck with a flashlight. Many drivers depend on their mechanics for preventative maintenance. When inspector McIlravy finds a problem that will put the truck out of service, he takes the time to show the driver the precise nature of the problem and explains why he is being put out of service. "Showing the driver what's wrong lets

A big rig driver covers around 500 miles a day. With that average, the driver of this conventional could cover one million miles in less than ten years.—© Bette S. Garber/Highway Images

the driver know that it's a serious problem," says McIlravy. "It also gives him the specific information he needs to communicate back to a mechanic and to his dispatcher."

A tractor or trailer that passes inspection is given a sticker. This sticker is good for 90 days of inspection-free driving anywhere in the country. The rig may still be inspected though, if an inspector sees something obviously wrong with the truck. It's a good system that works.

California Highway Patrol Sergeant, Gary Smith, the Facility Supervisor at the San Onofre, California, inspection facility on Interstate 5 says, "The average inspection takes 20 to 25 minutes. We realize that trucks are the blood stream of our society—time is money to truckers and we don't want to inconvenience the industry." Sergeant Smith went on to explain that the average truck, considering the number of miles it travels, is very safe. "I think our program is very effective," said Sergeant Smith. "The drivers are generally very cooperative. They realize that the inspection is for their benefit, as well as that of the general public. If something goes wrong with their truck, they're going down with it. Our aim is safety!"

Inspector McIlravy says he inspects between 10 and 16 trucks each day. "I find the people who drive the trucks are the best part of the job," says McIlravy. "Most of the drivers are great people with interesting stories to tell from the places they've traveled all over the country."

Winter Driving

Big rigs are driven in all types of weather, and winter driving presents a new set of challenges for the driver. In just a few days, a big rig may have traveled from the southwest desert into the frigid snow belt. These abrupt changes in climate require the big rig driver to plan the trip thoroughly and to prepare the equipment for the changes. Close attention to the condition of the tractor is paramount. All aspects of the cooling system must be checked regularly, especially anti-freeze levels

Sierra Pacific West driver, Willy Moss, attaches an OVERSIZE LOAD banner to the front bumper of his Peterbuilt prior to transporting a large piece of construction equipment. Before setting out on the road, he will scrape the loose dirt off of the dozer

Total weight of this tractor, trailer, and wheeled dozer is over 100,000 pounds, well above the 80,000 weight limit on big rigs. A load of this size is called a "permit load," because of the permit that must be obtained from the state highway department prior to moving something so large over public roads. This permit defines the roads to be traveled and the time of day to transport. Here the driver of the pilot vehicle is attaching red flags to the dozer's widest points, while the driver is chaining it down.

and hoses. Some operators change to a lighter weight gear lube in the winter. In bitterly cold areas, drivers put an additive in their diesel fuel to prevent gelling. Tire chains are required in many areas when it snows and they must be maintained. Drivers must remember to carry tire chains, keep them in proper working order, and know how to install them.

Drivers must also prepare themselves for survival in cold climates. They need to pack a heavy jacket, boots, and gloves in case they're stranded and need to go out in extremely cold weather to repair their rig. Food and water for survival is another con-

sideration if stranded in a winter storm. The well-prepared driver will pack non-perishable canned and dried foods in the cab.

Driving a big rig in snow is not much different from driving in rain. The professional trucker will always match the speed to the conditions. "The bottom line to any inclement weather—slow down," says Jim Dancy, Director of Market Development for the United States Truck driving School. "No company safety office will fail to back a driver if he didn't feel safe." If the road conditions get too bad to continue, the experienced driver will shut down. No customer wants his load in a ditch.

Loading something as large as this wheeled dozer onto a low bed trailer takes a high degree of skill. Because the width of the dozer is wider than the trailer, he must insure that it's balanced side to side.

Willy Moss has been driving big rigs since 1970. Most of his driving career has been spent hauling oversized heavy equipment. Moss says that when carrying loads that are heavier and larger than normal, he must anticipate anything that can possibly happen as far ahead as possible. Good advice for any driver!

When transporting freshly cut trees, the trucks must go into the woods to pick up the load. This usually means traveling on dirt roads or simple paths cut through the woods.—*Caterpillar Engine Division/Paul Harder*

Previous Page
The trailer used to transport logs is called a pole trailer. The beam below the logs is the telescopic section that connects the front and rear portions of the trailer. Securely chaining the logs together prior to transport is very important. Here a lumber jack is laying his weight into a snap binder to tighten the load.—

Right
Following a successful inspection, the old sticker is removed and a new one put in its place. These stickers are good for three months of inspection-free driving. When the sticker expires, the truck may be stopped at any time for another inspection. A typical inspection takes about 20 minutes and is focused on safety.

This is why truck inspectors are called "creeper cops." While conducting checks under trucks and trailers, the inspectors wear hard hats (the brim has been removed on this inspector's hat) and safety glasses. Here the inspector is checking the air brake system on a trailer.

Truck inspections are done as much for the big rig driver as they are for the safety of the driving public. These inspectors are trained to find safety defects the average driver may not detect. Here the inspector is checking the draw bar connection between trailers. Banks of lights imbedded in the paved inspection area illuminate the underside of the tractor and trailer.

Breakdowns on the road happen to even the best maintained rigs. When they do occur, the tow truck needed to haul an 80,000 pound tractor-trailer combination needs to be strong and powerful. This Caterpillar-powered Peterbuilt tow truck has been custom built to tow big rigs.

Communications

When we think of communication gear in a big rig, we automatically think of CB (Citizens Band) radios. Truckers use their CB radios and still have their "handles" (nick names). CB radios are an extremely effective means of communication between trucks traveling the same stretch of highway.

Messages can be relayed through other truckers on the road concerning traffic problems miles ahead. Drivers can then select another route to stay on schedule. Truckers are always eager to help out one another. One trucker said, "Even though you may have directions to your destination, you may have been diverted or made a wrong turn. All you need to do is get on the CB and state what you're looking for, and bang—someone will be there to help you."

In the cabs of many trucks today is a cell phone. The cell phone enables the driver to talk directly to the dispatcher. It's also a very useful tool to enable the driver to communicate with the destination in case there is an unforeseen delay in delivery.

Truck Stops

Dotting the landscape across America are truck stops—safe havens for truckers. These islands of refuge are located in every state, usually near the intersection of two interstate highways. Open 24-hours a day, 365 days a year, truck stops offer everything a trucker needs while on the road. The names of these stops run from the obvious, like the *Exit 3 Truck Stop* in Paducha, Kentucky (to get there you take exit 3 off of I-24), to the more inventive and unusual, like *Lottie's Smoking Club* in Rialto, California; *Tank-N-Tummy* in Madison, Florida; *Fat Harvey's* in Canyonville, Oregon; *Cruel Jack's* in Rock Springs, Wyoming; or *Whiskey Pete's Casino/ Truck Stop* in Jean, Nevada. If you're traveling through Wisconsin on US-2, you may want to get off at exit 10 in the city of Poplar. There you'll find *Mother's Kitchen*, where all the food is homemade— "no instant spuds or canned gravy here!"

Huge quantities of food is one of the features of a truck stop. Truckers take their eating seriously and want good food and lots of it. The truck stop menu is all-American. It's doubtful you'll find sushi at a truck stop, but if steak, cheeseburgers, or hearty ham and eggs are your pleasure, a truck stop is the place to eat. The *Eagle Landing Truck Stop* in Matthews, Missouri (I-55, exit 58) offers a gigantic 24-ounce hamburger. But, that's small potatoes compared to the four-pound Big Max Burger offered at the *Bosselman Travel Center* in Grand Island, Nebraska (I-80, exit 312). If you're man or woman enough to try, and can finish it within an hour, they'll give you a T-shirt and take your picture.

Waitresses serving the food at truck stops are often as colorful as the truckers themselves. Requirements to be a good truck stop waitress are: always have coffee ready; provide fast service; have a pleasant smile; and maintain a sharp wit. For those truckers who want to eat in a hurry, many truck stops offer a large buffet for those drivers who want to pile their plates high with tasty food.

Truck stops also offer showers where the weary driver can get freshened-up for another stint behind the wheel; or they can stop in the lounge and catch up on the latest news on televisions tuned to CNN. Truck repair facilities and fuel are available, too. Truck stops have it all for the big rig driver on the road.

This Komatsu bulldozer came straight from the ship, which transported it from Japan to Oakland, California, to the trailer of this truck. Also, stacked four high on the deck of the ship are shipping containers that will eventually be transported by truck.—*Willy Moss*

Many drivers carry pagers. A pay phone is always within a 30-minute drive.

The use of cell phones to communicate with a dispatcher or with family can be rather expensive. Also, there are some areas of the country where there are gaps in the cellular system. A new technology used by truck fleets is a system that keeps the driver in constant contact with a dispatcher and can even be used by the driver to communicate with his family via the Internet. Probably the most advanced system for this type of real-time communication is Qualcomm's OmniTRACS® satellite system. OmniTRACS® is an integrated communications tool that links the truck on the road to the dispatch center via satellite link. It is composed of a heavy-duty in-cab display unit, a communications unit (the black box), and an external antenna.

Following loading, this salt truck has stopped at the scales to be weighed prior to hitting the road. If he were overweight and stopped at a state inspection station, the driver would need to adjust his weight down to the legal limit (80,000 pounds) prior to continuing.— *Fred Pushies*

The OmniTRACS® in-cab display unit is about the size of a laptop computer. It weighs just under three pounds, has a full keyboard, numeric pad, and a 4-line by 40 character backlit display. An optional display is available that offers 15 lines of 40 characters, backlit soft-touch keys, and several other features. The brains of the system is the communications unit. It's housed in an aluminum case measuring 12.8"x9.2"x2.9" and weighs only seven pounds. Its maximum message size is 1900 characters and the unit has enough memory to hold 99 messages, or 600 lines. This system is made possible by Qualcomm's development of an innovative antenna design that uses the proprietary Ku-band. The antenna, circular in shape (11.5" diameter x 6.75"), mounts externally, usually on top of the sleeper's fairing. An electronically-driven motor keeps the antenna aligned with the satellite at all times. This antenna permits error-free transmission of data and a high degree of reliability.

Unlike cell phone communication, a driver using a satellite based system is never out of touch with the dispatcher. The driver can always be contacted with new instructions on deliveries and pick-ups. The driver can also obtain route information. Route information is programmed by each individual dispatch location for the routes they most often use. The OmniTRACS® can accept driver data input from other peripherals, such as a bar code scanner or personal computer. An additional option to the OmniTRACS® system, Cab-CARD®, is one which allows the driver to send and receive e-mail messages over the Internet. The driver away from home can catch up on his daughter's soccer scores and send back congratulations for the goals she scored.

Haulin' Coast to Coast

I asked long-haul driver Barb Jasper to describe the typical events that happen when hauling a load of vegetables coast to coast. Barb, along with her long-time friend, Diane Danka, drives a magenta-colored Freightliner for Prime Inc. out of Missouri. "We will usually get a message on our Qualcomm that will tell us to go to Salinas, California, for a load of vegetables for the Hunts Market in New York. While the produce is being loaded, we will "pulp" it (take the temperature with a probe thermometer). We need to be sure it's not frozen or too warm. We always stand outside the trailer and watch the load. Most of the dock workers load correctly, but there have been a few times when we made them take everything out and reload it. The typical load may have both fruit and vegetables. We will usually load the vegetables first, then add the fruit, so it's in the center of the trailer where the temperature is the most stable. Then we fill in the rear with more vegetables. The entire loading process may take from four to twelve hours. It takes longer when the produce to be shipped is still being picked in the field. After the produce is in the trailer, we put our load locks across the top to keep it down in case we hit a big bump. We also put load locks across the ends to keep it from shifting. Once the trailer is fully loaded, we lock the doors and duct tape the pulp thermometer to the inside of the small door that's on one of the large rear doors. This gives us the ability to double check the reefer unit's output to be sure of the trailer's internal temperature."

While the load is going on, they will "punch up" the trip on the Qualcomm OmniTRACS® system. They input an 01 (loading location) and a 90 (their destination). The system will display a suggested, shortest route. They compare that route with their maps to avoid any bad weather. Prior to leaving, they eat a full meal. Diane prefers to drive at night and Barb likes to drive during the day. If they've both been up most of the day loading, they flip a coin to see who starts. If Diane starts, she'll drive an eight-hour shift and Barb will climb into the sleeper. About four hours into the drive, Diane will stop for fuel and "check the pulp." She will open the small door on the back of the trailer and check the thermometer to monitor the temperature. At the end of eight hours Diane and Barb will find a place to eat. They try to avoid truck stops, since most of this food is fried and just doesn't agree with them. They often stop in a mall or find another small restaurant along the road. Once back in the truck, Diane will climb into the sleeper and Barb will drive her eight-hour shift. It's a three day drive from Salinas, California, to New York. When they arrive in New York, the Qualcomm OmniTRACS® system gives them exact directions, including landmarks, number of stoplights, and which way to turn. They've never been late with a load.

Unloading takes about one to one and a half hours. The receiver checks the temperature of the produce prior to ac-

cepting it. Some check with a thermometer, while some experienced veterans can tell by feel if it's the proper temperature.

"In New York we may get a Qualcomm message that will have us go to New Jersey to pick up a FedEx load for Memphis," Barb explains. "When you deliver for FedEx, you must deliver on time and let them know where you are along the way. The Qualcomm message may say 'you have 12 hours to get to Memphis and you must check in every five hours.' The FedEx folks advertise that they can tell a customer where their package is. That's why we're required to check in."

Barb Jasper loves truck driving because it allows her to travel the country. "I've got daughters in Illinois, Florida, and California. Instead of seeing one of them two weeks out of a year, I get to see everyone one of them at least three times a year." She also carries a video camcorder and records her travels to share with her grandchildren. "Where else can you see the United States and get paid for it!"

Driving a big rig is no longer a male-dominated occupation. Approximately 30 percent of today's truckers are women. Barb Jasper (left) and Diane Dakan, AKA "Thelma and Louise," are former restaurant workers who transitioned to big rigs. Together they average 200,000 miles a year in their magenta-colored Freightliner. They typically haul refrigerated goods cross-country. Barb videotapes their journeys for her grandchildren. The tattoo on Diane's left shoulder is of—what else—a magenta Freightliner.—© Bette S. Garber/Highway Images

Right
Bad weather is only one of the challenges today's truck driver faces. The first piece of advice a new driver receives about driving in bad weather is to slow down. And, if he still feels uncomfortable, he should pull over and stop. Shippers would rather have their load a day late, than to hear that it has been damaged in a weather related traffic accident.—© Bette S. Garber/Highway Images

Index